Cambridge Latin Course

Unit 1

FIFTH EDITION

CAMBRIDGE
UNIVERSITY PRESS

University Printing House, Cambridge CB2 8BS, United Kingdom

One Liberty Plaza, 20th Floor, New York, NY 10006, USA

477 Williamstown Road, Port Melbourne, VIC 3207, Australia

4843/24, 2nd Floor, Ansari Road, Daryaganj, Delhi – 110002, India

79 Anson Road, #06–04/06, Singapore 079906

Cambridge University Press is part of the University of Cambridge.

It furthers the University's mission by disseminating knowledge in the pursuit of education, learning and research at the highest international levels of excellence.

Information on this title: education.cambridge.org

The Cambridge Latin Course is an outcome of work jointly commissioned by the Cambridge School Classics Project and the Schools Council © Schools Council 1970, 1982 (succeeded by the School Curriculum Development Committee © SCDC Publications 1988).

© University of Cambridge School Classics Project 2001, 2015

First published 1970
Second edition 1982
Third edition 1988
Fourth edition 2001
Fifth edition 2015
Reprinted 2016

Printed in the United States of America

Library of Congress Cataloging in Publication Data

Data available

ISBN 978-1-107-07093-6 Hardback
ISBN 978-1-107-48465-8 Hardback +6 Year Website Access
ISBN 978-1-107-48437-5 Hardback +1 Year Website Access
ISBN 978-1-107-69063-9 Paperback
ISBN 978-1-107-48461-0 Paperback +1 Year Websute Access

Cover image, Ministero per i Beni e le Attività Culturali, background, Semisatch / Shutterstock
Maps and plans by Robert Calow / Eikon
Illustrations by Joy Mellor, Leslie Jones, Peter Kesteven, Neil Sutton, and Lisa Jiang.

Cambridge University Press has no responsibility for the persistence or accuracy of URLs for external or third-party internet websites referred to in this publication, and does not guarantee that any content on such websites is, or will remain, accurate or appropriate. Information regarding prices, travel timetables, and other factual information given in this work is correct at the time of first printing but Cambridge University Press does not guarantee the accuracy of such information thereafter.

Contents

Acknowledgments

The authors and publishers acknowledge the following sources of copyright material and are grateful for the permissions granted. While every effort has been made, it has not always been possible to identify the sources of all the material used, or to trace all copyright holders. If any omissions are brought to our notice, we will be happy to include the appropriate acknowledgments on reprinting.

pp. 1, 8 *t*, 9 *tr*, 12 *tr*, 13 *bl*, 26, 35 *t*, 36, 37 *c*, 38, 43, 46, 48, 51 *tl*, 51 *cl (No. 2)*, 51 *cl (No. 4)*, 51 *bl*, 64 *b*, 65 *t*, 82, 96 *br*, 119, 127 *tl*, 127 *br*, 129, 147, 153, 155, 159 *t*, 160 *b*, 162, 169 *l*, 171 *all images*, 176 *t*, Ministero per i Beni e le Attività Culturali; pp. 9*bl*, *cl*, 47 *r*, 58 *l*, *r*, Museo Archeologico Nazionale, Naples; p. 10, Bridgeman Art Library, Head of a Roman Lady, Flavian Period, Late 1st century AD (marble); pp. 14 *tl*, *tr*, *bl*, *br*, 67 *bl*, 79 *br*, p 111 *shield*, 141, 163, ©The British Museum; p. 15, ©Metropolitan Museum of Art, New York, Rogers Fund, 1903 (03.13.13). Photograph by Schechter Lee; pp. 21, 25 *cl*, 37, 51 *cr*, 96 *bl*, 97, 111 (*neck guard and greave*), 124, 125, 126, 127 *cl*, 130, CSCP; p. 36 *bl* ©Peter Landon / Alamy; pp. 36–37 (background), ©Jackie and Bob Dunn www.pompeiiinpictures.com. Su concessione del Ministero per i Beni e le Attività Culturali: Soprintendenza Speciale per i Beni Archeologici di Napoli e Pompei; p 44 *l*, ©Fitzwilliam Museum, University of Cambridge; pp. 44 *ct*, 169 *r*, V&A Images/©Victoria and Albert Museum; p. 49 *br* National Geographic Image Collection/Alamy; p. 51 *br*, from The Garden of Pompeii by W. F. Jashemsky (Caratzas Bros, NY); p. 67 Visual Publications; p. 69 Musée royal du Mariemont; p. 93 Getty Images p. 112 JMN/Getty Images; p. 131 Giraudon (Bridgeman Art Library); p. 143 ©The British Library Board; p. 173 Yale Centre for British Art; p. 176 O. Louis Mazzatenta/ National Geographic Creative

All other photography by R.L. Dalladay.

The current edition of the *Cambridge Latin Course* is the result of over forty years of research, classroom testing, feedback, revision, and development. In that period millions of students, tens of thousands of teachers, hundreds of experts in the fields of Classics, history, and education, and dozens of authors have contributed to make the Course the leading approach to reading Latin that it is today.

To list everyone who has played a part in the development of the *Cambridge Latin Course* would be impossible, but we would particularly like to thank individuals and representatives from the following organizations, past and present:

British Museum
British School at Rome
Butser Ancient Farm, England
Castell Henllys, Wales
Council for British Archaeology
Department of Education and Science, London
Fishbourne Palace, England
Herculaneum Conservation Project
Her Majesty's Inspectorate of Schools
North American Cambridge Classics Project
Nuffield Foundation
Qualifications and Curriculum Authority, London
Queen Mary University of London, Department of Classics
Schools Council, London
Southern Universities Joint Board for School Examinations, England
St Matthias College of Education, Bristol
Swedish Pompeii Project
University of Bradford, Department of Classics
University of Cambridge, Faculty of Classics
University of Cambridge, Faculty of Education
University of Cambridge School Classics Project Advisory Panel
University College Cardiff, Classics Department
University College London, Centre for the History of Medicine
University College London, Department of Greek and Latin
University of Leeds, Department of Classics
University of Leeds, School of Education
University of London, Institute of Education
University of Manchester, Department of Art History and Visual Studies
University of Massachusetts at Amherst, Department of Classics
University of Nottingham, Department of Classics
University of Nottingham, School of Education
University of Oxford, Department of Education
University of Oxford, Faculty of Classics
University of Oxford, School of Archaeology
University of Wales, School of Archaeology, History and Anthropology
University of Warwick, Classics Department
Welsh Joint Education Committee

CAECILIUS

Stage 1

familia

1   Caecilius est pater.

2   Metella est māter.

3   Quīntus est fīlius.

4   Lūcia est fīlia.

5   Clēmēns est servus.

6   Grumiō est coquus.

7   Cerberus est canis.

8   Caecilius est in tablīnō.

9   Metella est in ātriō.

10   Quīntus est in triclīniō.

11   Lūcia est in hortō.

12   Clēmēns est in cubiculō.

13   Grumiō est in culīnā.

14   Cerberus est in viā.

15 pater est in tablīnō.
    pater in tablīnō scrībit.

16 māter est in ātriō.
    māter in ātriō sedet.

17 fīlius est in triclīniō.
    fīlius in triclīniō bibit.

18 fīlia est in hortō.
    fīlia in hortō legit.

19 servus est in cubiculō.
    servus in cubiculō labōrat.

20 coquus est in culīnā.
    coquus in culīnā labōrat.

21 canis est in viā.
    canis in viā dormit.

Vocabulary

familia	*household*	**in tablīnō**	*in the study*	**scrībit**	*is writing*
est	*is*	**in ātriō**	*in the atrium*	**sedet**	*is sitting*
pater	*father*		*(main room)*	**bibit**	*is drinking*
māter	*mother*	**in triclīniō**	*in the dining room*	**legit**	*is reading*
fīlius	*son*	**in hortō**	*in the garden*	**labōrat**	*is working*
fīlia	*daughter*	**in cubiculō**	*in the bedroom*	**dormit**	*is sleeping*
servus	*slave*	**in culīnā**	*in the kitchen*		
coquus	*cook*	**in viā**	*in the street*		
canis	*dog*				

Cerberus

Caecilius est in hortō. Caecilius in hortō sedet. Lūcia est in hortō. Lūcia in hortō legit. servus est in ātriō. servus in ātriō labōrat. Metella est in ātriō. Metella in ātriō sedet. Quīntus est in tablīnō. Quīntus in tablīnō scrībit. Cerberus est in viā.

Caecilius had this mosaic of a dog in the doorway of his house.

coquus est in culīnā. coquus in culīnā dormit. Cerberus intrat. 5
Cerberus circumspectat. cibus est in mēnsā. canis salit. canis in mēnsā stat. Grumiō stertit. canis lātrat. Grumiō surgit. coquus est īrātus. "pestis! furcifer!" coquus clāmat. Cerberus exit.

intrat *enters*
circumspectat *looks around*
cibus *food*
in mēnsā *on the table*
salit *jumps*
stat *stands*
stertit *snores*
lātrat *barks*
surgit *gets up*
īrātus *angry*
pestis! *pest!*
furcifer! *scoundrel!*
clāmat *shouts*
exit *goes out*

About the language

1 Latin sentences containing the word **est** often have the same order as English. For example:

    Metella est māter.   canis est in viā.
    Metella is the mother.   *The dog is in the street.*

2 In other Latin sentences, the order is usually different from that of English. For example:

    canis in viā dormit.   servus in culīnā labōrat.
    The dog is sleeping in the street.   *The slave is working in the kitchen.*

3 Note that **dormit** and **labōrat** in the sentences above can be translated in another way. For example: **servus in culīnā labōrat** can mean *The slave works in the kitchen* as well as *The slave is working in the kitchen*. The story will help you to decide which translation gives the better sense.

Practicing the language

Write out each Latin sentence, completing it with a suitable word or phrase from the box. Then translate the sentence. Use each word or phrase only once.

    For example: .... est in cubiculō.
           servus est in cubiculō.
           The slave is in the bedroom.

1

Lūcia	Grumiō	Caecilius
canis	māter	servus	filius

2

in viā	in hortō	in ātriō	in tablīnō
in culīnā	in triclīniō	in cubiculō	

1
a .... est in cubiculō.
b .... est in hortō.
c .... est in viā.
d .... est in culīnā.
e .... est in tablīnō.
f .... est in ātriō.
g .... est in triclīniō.

2
a Clēmēns .... labōrat.
b Caecilius .... scrībit.
c canis .... lātrat.
d Metella .... stat.
e Lūcia est ....
f coquus est ....
g Quīntus est ....

Caecilius

Caecilius lived in Italy during the first century AD in the town of Pompeii. The town was situated at the foot of Mount Vesuvius on the coast of the Bay of Naples, and may have had a population of about 10,000. Caecilius was a rich Pompeian banker. When archaeologists excavated his house they discovered his accounts in a strongbox. These documents tell us that he was also an auctioneer, tax collector, farmer, and moneylender.

He inherited some of his money, but he probably made most of it through shrewd and energetic business activities. He dealt in slaves, cloth, timber, and property. He also ran a laundry and dyeing business, grazed sheep and cattle on pastureland outside the town, and he sometimes won the contract for collecting the local taxes. He may have owned a few shops as well, and probably lent money to local shipping companies wishing to trade with countries overseas. The profit on such trading was often very large.

The front of Caecilius' house. The spaces on either side of the door were shops he probably owned.

A laundry like this was among his business interests.

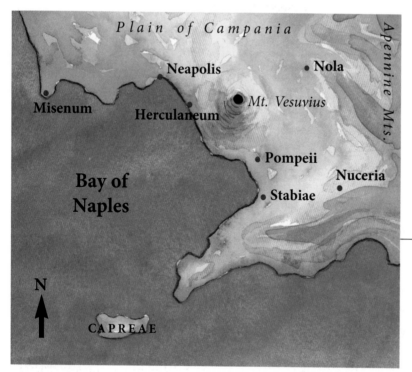

The Bay of Naples (Neapolis). The area covered by this map is about 40 miles (60 kilometers) wide.

Central and southern Italy.

Caecilius' full name was Lucius Caecilius Iucundus. Lucius was his personal name, rather like a modern first name. His second name, Caecilius, shows that he was a member of the "clan" of the Caecilii. Clans or groups of families were very important and strong feelings of loyalty existed within them. Caecilius' third name, Iucundus, is the name of his own family and close relatives. The word **iūcundus** means "pleasant" just as in English we find surnames like Merry or Jolly.

Only a Roman citizen would have three names. A slave would have just one, such as Clemens or Grumio. As a Roman citizen, Caecilius not only had the right to vote in elections, but also was fully protected by the law against unjust treatment. The slaves who lived and worked in his house and in his businesses had no rights of their own. They were his property and he could treat them well or badly as he wished. There was one important exception to this rule. The law did not allow a master to put a slave to death without showing good reason.

This head found in Caecilius' house may be a portrait of him.

This is one of the wooden tablets found in Caecilius' house. They recorded his business dealings. The writing was on wax in the central recess and when the tablets were discovered much of the writing could still be read. The tablets were tied together in twos or threes through the holes at the top.

One page of the writing: it records the sale at auction of a slave for 6,252 sesterces.

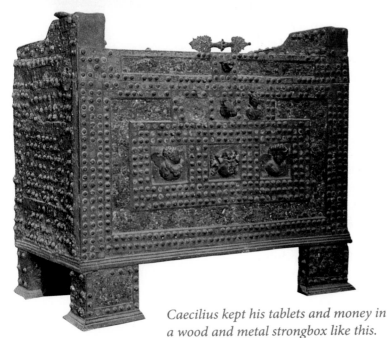

Caecilius kept his tablets and money in a wood and metal strongbox like this.

Roman coins: a bronze sestertius, a silver denarius, and a gold aureus.

Metella

There is much less evidence available from the Roman world about women than there is about men, so what we know about Roman women is limited. For example, we know that Caecilius had at least two sons, Quintus and Sextus, but we do not know the name of their mother. Therefore we have imagined the character of Metella who appears in our stories as the wife of Caecilius.

A Roman girl was traditionally named after her father's clan. If Metella had been a real person, her name would indicate that she was a member of the clan of the Metelli. Similarly, a daughter of Caecilius would have been known as Caecilia. Sisters were distinguished by the addition of a second name, sometimes taken from a family member. We have imagined Caecilius' daughter to be Caecilia Lucia.

Romans did not expect women to have the same rights as men. A woman like Metella did not have full control over her own life. Her father would choose her husband, usually an older man, and she may have had little say in the decision. She would normally be married by the age of twenty, and daughters in upper-class or very rich families were sometimes given in marriage as young as twelve. At the time of our stories, the law gave most fathers control over their daughters, even after the daughter was married.

Yet Metella's role was an important one. Her main duty in her marriage would have been to produce children and help bring them up. A woman like Metella may have had ten or twelve children, only some of whom would have survived to adulthood. She was also responsible for the management of the large household, and had to supervise the work of the domestic slaves. In order to run the household successfully, she would need to be well organized, and firm but sensitive in her control of the slaves.

Women's hairstyles were often very elaborate. Many women were rich enough to own slave hairdressers.

Houses in Pompeii

The house in which a wealthy man like Caecilius lived differed in several ways from an equivalent house today. The house came right up to the sidewalk; there was no garden or grass in front of it. The windows were few, small, and placed fairly high up. They were intended to let in enough light, but to keep out the heat of the sun. Large windows would have made the rooms uncomfortably hot in summer and cold in winter.

Plan of a Pompeian house

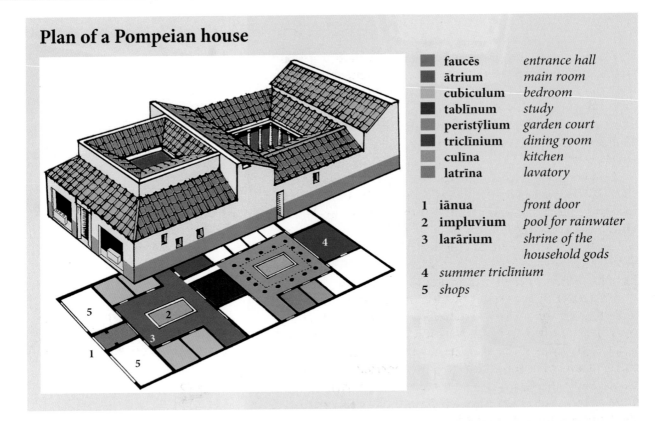

■	**faucēs**	*entrance hall*
■	**ātrium**	*main room*
■	**cubiculum**	*bedroom*
■	**tablīnum**	*study*
■	**peristȳlium**	*garden court*
■	**triclīnium**	*dining room*
■	**culīna**	*kitchen*
■	**latrīna**	*lavatory*

1	**iānua**	*front door*
2	**impluvium**	*pool for rainwater*
3	**larārium**	*shrine of the household gods*
4		*summer triclīnium*
5		*shops*

Most houses stood only one story high, although some had a second floor above. Many had shops on either side of the main door, which were rented out by the owner of the house. From the outside, with its few windows and high walls stretching all the way around, the house did not look very attractive or inviting.

The floor plan of the house shows two parts or areas of about equal size. They look like courtyards surrounded by rooms opening off the central space.

The main entrance to the house was on the side facing the street. It consisted of a tall double door. The Latin word for this door was **iānua**. On passing through the door, the visitor came into a short corridor which led straight into the main room, the **ātrium**. This impressive room, which was used for important family occasions and for receiving visitors, was large and high. The roof sloped down slightly toward a large square opening called the **compluvium**. The light streamed in through the opening high overhead. Immediately below was the **impluvium**, a shallow rectangular pool, lined with marble, which collected the rainwater.

In what ways is this house typical of houses in Caecilius' day?

The atrium in Caecilius' house as it is today. We can see how spacious it was, but for a real sense of the dignity of an atrium we need to look at a better-preserved one (left). The visitor entering the front door would see, beyond the impluvium, the tablinum and the sunlit peristylium beyond.

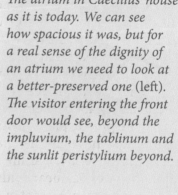

A lararium.

One of the most striking things about the atrium was the sense of space. The high roof with the glimpse of the sky through the central opening and the large floor area helped to give this impression. The furniture would include a bronze or marble table, a couch, and perhaps a strongbox in which the family valuables were stored. In a corner, near the main door, was the **larārium**, a small shrine at which the family gods were worshipped. The floor of the atrium was paved with marble slabs or sometimes with mosaics. The walls were decorated with panels of brightly painted plaster. The Pompeians were especially fond of red, orange, and blue. On many of these panels there were scenes from well-known stories, especially the Greek myths.

Around the atrium were arranged the bedrooms, study, and dining room. The entrances to these rooms were usually provided not with a wooden door but with a heavy curtain.

From this first area of the house, the visitor walked through the **tablīnum** (study), or a passage, into the second part. This was the **peristȳlium**, which was made up of a colonnade of pillars surrounding the **hortus** (garden). Like the atrium, the colonnade was often elaborately decorated. Around the outside of the colonnade were the summer dining room, kitchen, lavatory, slaves' quarters, and storage rooms. Some houses also had their own set of baths.

The garden was laid out with flowers and shrubs in a careful plan. In the small fishpond in the middle, a fountain threw up a jet of water, and marble statues of gods and heroes stood here and there. In the peristylium, the members of the family enjoyed the sunshine or shade as they wished; here they relaxed on their own or entertained their guests.

The Pompeians not only lived in houses that looked very different from modern ones, but also thought very differently about them. They did not expect their houses to be private places restricted to the family and close friends. Instead, the master conducted much of his business and social life from home. He would receive and do business with most visitors in the atrium. The more important ones would be invited into the tablinum. Certain very close business friends and high-ranking individuals would receive invitations to dine or relax in the peristylium with the family.

Even if there were no outsiders present, the members of the family were never on their own. They were surrounded and often outnumbered by their slaves. They did not attach as much importance to privacy as many people do today.

Only the wealthy lived like this; most people lived in much simpler homes. Some of the poorer shopkeepers, for instance, would have had only a room or two above their shops. In large cities such as Rome, many people lived in apartment buildings several stories high, some of them in very poor conditions.

Caecilius' tablinum was decorated with vibrant colors, including a particularly expensive shade of red paint.

A painting of a marble fountain in a garden.

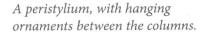

A peristylium, with hanging ornaments between the columns.

Vocabulary checklist 1

canis	*dog*
coquus	*cook*
est	*is*
fīlia	*daughter*
fīlius	*son*
hortus	*garden*
in	*in*
labōrat	*works, is working*
māter	*mother*
pater	*father*
sedet	*sits, is sitting*
servus	*slave*
via	*street*

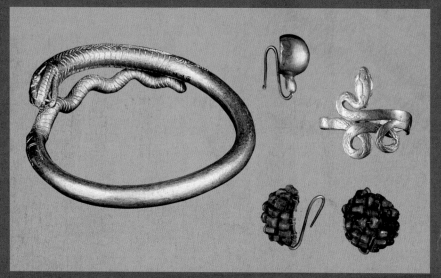

Many wealthy Roman women were very fond of jewelry. Here are some examples of the things they might have worn.

IN VILLA

Stage 2

amīcus

1 Caecilius est in ātriō.

2 amīcus Caecilium salūtat.

5   Lūcia est in ātriō.

6   amīcus Lūciam salūtat.

7   servus est in ātriō.

8   amīcus servum salūtat.

9   canis est in ātriō.

10   amīcus canem salūtat.

Metella

11 coquus est in culīnā.

12 Metella culīnam intrat.

13 Grumiō labōrat.

14 Metella Grumiōnem spectat.

15 cibus est parātus.

16 Metella cibum gustat.

17 Grumiō est anxius.

18 Metella Grumiōnem laudat.

19 amīcus est in hortō.

20 Metella amīcum vocat.

mercātor

amīcus Caecilium vīsitat. amīcus est mercātor. mercātor vīllam
intrat. Clēmēns est in ātriō. Clēmēns mercātōrem salūtat.
Caecilius est in tablīnō. Caecilius pecūniam numerat. Caecilius
est argentārius. amīcus tablīnum intrat. Caecilius surgit.
 "salvē!" Caecilius mercātōrem salūtat.   5
 "salvē!" mercātor respondet.
 Caecilius triclīnium intrat. amīcus quoque intrat. amīcus in
lectō recumbit. argentārius in lectō recumbit.
 Grumiō in culīnā cantat. Grumiō pāvōnem coquit. coquus est
laetus. Caecilius coquum audit. Caecilius nōn est laetus.   10
Caecilius cēnam exspectat. amīcus cēnam exspectat. Caecilius
Grumiōnem vituperat.

mercātor *merchant*

amīcus *friend*
vīsitat *is visiting*
vīllam *house*
salūtat *greets*
pecūniam numerat
    is counting money
argentārius *banker*
salvē! *hello!*
respondet *replies*
quoque *also*
in lectō recumbit
    reclines on a couch
cantat *is singing*
pāvōnem *peacock*
coquit *is cooking*
laetus *happy*
audit *hears, listens to*
nōn est *is not*
cēnam *dinner*
exspectat *is waiting for*
vituperat *tells off, curses*

in triclīniō

Grumiō triclīnium intrat. Grumiō pāvōnem portat. Clēmēns
triclīnium intrat. Clēmēns vīnum portat. Caecilius pāvōnem
gustat.
 "pāvō est optimus!" Caecilius clāmat.
mercātor quoque pāvōnem gustat. mercātor cēnam laudat.   5
dominus coquum laudat. Grumiō exit.
 ancilla intrat. ancilla suāviter cantat. ancilla dominum
dēlectat. ancilla mercātōrem dēlectat. mox dominus dormit.
amīcus quoque dormit.
 Grumiō triclīnium intrat et circumspectat. coquus cibum in   10
mēnsā videt. Grumiō cibum cōnsūmit et vīnum bibit! Caecilius
Grumiōnem nōn videt. coquus in triclīniō magnificē cēnat.
 coquus ancillam spectat. ancilla Grumiōnem dēlectat.
Grumiō ancillam dēlectat. Grumiō est laetissimus.

portat *is carrying*
vīnum *wine*
gustat *tastes*
optimus *very good, excellent*
laudat *praises*
dominus *master*
ancilla *slave girl*
suāviter *sweetly*
dēlectat *pleases*
mox *soon*
et *and*
videt *sees*
cibum cōnsūmit *eats the food*
magnificē *magnificently,
    in style*
cēnat *eats dinner, dines*
spectat *looks at*
laetissimus *very happy*

About the language

1 Words like **Metella**, **Caecilius**, and **mercātor** are known as **nouns**.
 They often indicate people or animals (e.g. **ancilla** and **canis**), places
 (e.g. **vīlla**, **hortus**), and things (e.g. **cēna**, **cibus**).

2 You have now met two forms of the same noun:

 Metella – Metellam
 Caecilius – Caecilium
 mercātor – mercātōrem

3 The different forms are known as the **nominative case** and the
 accusative case.

nominative	Metella	Caecilius	mercātor
accusative	Metellam	Caecilium	mercātōrem

4 If Metella does something, such as praising Grumio,
 the nominative **Metella** is used:

 Metella Grumiōnem laudat.
 Metella praises Grumio.

5 But if somebody else does something to Metella,
 the accusative **Metellam** is used:

 amīcus **Metellam** salūtat.
 The friend greets Metella.

6 Notice again the difference in word order
 between Latin and English:

 coquus culīnam intrat.
 The cook enters the kitchen.

 Clēmēns vīnum portat.
 Clemens carries the wine.

Peacocks often figured on Pompeian wall paintings as well as on their dinner tables.

Practicing the language

1 Write out each Latin sentence, completing it with a suitable word or phrase from the box. Then translate the sentence. Use each phrase only once.

> For example: canis . . . . stat.
> canis **in viā** stat.
> *The dog is standing in the street.*

scrībit	in culīnā
servus	amīcus
sedet	in viā

a Grumiō . . . . coquit.
b . . . . in cubiculō labōrat.
c mercātor in tablīnō . . . .

d Cerberus . . . . dormit.
e Metella in ātriō . . . .
f . . . . in triclīniō cēnat.

2 Write out each Latin sentence, completing it with the correct word from the parentheses. Then translate the sentence.

> For example: amīcus Caecilium . . . . (sedet, vīsitat)
> amīcus Caecilium **vīsitat**.
> *A friend visits Caecilius.*

a Caecilius pecūniam . . . . (numerat, dormit)
b Clēmēns vīnum . . . . (labōrat, portat)
c ancilla hortum . . . . (intrat, gustat)
d Metella mercātōrem . . . . (salūtat, cantat)
e Quīntus cibum . . . . (vīsitat, cōnsūmit)
f Lūcia vīllam . . . . (dormit, intrat, portat)
g amīcus Grumiōnem . . . . (spectat, stat, recumbit)
h māter fīlium . . . . (bibit, dormit, vituperat)
i mercātor canem . . . . (sedet, cōnsūmit, audit)
j dominus ancillam . . . . (scrībit, laudat, numerat)

3 Translate this story:

amīcus

amīcus Grumiōnem vīsitat. amīcus est servus. servus
vīllam intrat. Clēmēns est in ātriō. servus Clēmentem
videt. Clēmēns servum salūtat. servus culīnam intrat.
servus culīnam circumspectat.
  Grumiō nōn est in culīnā. servus cibum videt. cibus   5
est parātus! servus cibum gustat. cibus est optimus.   **parātus** *ready*
  Grumiō culīnam intrat. Grumiō amīcum videt.
amīcus cibum cōnsūmit! coquus est īrātus.
  "pestis! furcifer!" coquus clāmat. coquus amīcum
vituperat.   *10*

Daily life

The day began early for Caecilius and the members of his household. He would usually get up at dawn. His slaves were up even earlier, sweeping, dusting, and polishing.

It did not take Caecilius long to dress. The first garment that he put on was his tunic, similar to a short-sleeved shirt, then his **toga**, a very large piece of woolen cloth arranged in folds, and finally his shoes, which were rather like modern sandals. A quick wash of the hands and face with cold water was enough at that time of the morning. Later he would visit a barber and be shaved, and in the afternoon he would enjoy a leisurely visit to the public baths.

His wife, Metella, also got up early. She would put on a **stola**, a full-length tunic. If she was going out, she would also wear a large rectangular shawl. With the help of a skilled slave woman, she did her hair in the latest style, put on her make-up, including powder, rouge, and mascara, and arranged her jewelry, of which she would have had a large and varied collection.

Breakfast was only a light snack, often just a cup of water and a piece of bread. The first duty of the day for Caecilius was to receive the respectful greetings of a number of poorer people and freedmen who had previously been his slaves. He would receive these visitors in the atrium and hand out small sums of money to them. If they were in any kind of trouble, he gave them as much help and protection as he could. In return, they helped Caecilius in several ways. For example, they accompanied him as a group of supporters on public occasions, and they might also be employed by him in business affairs. They were known as his **clientēs**, and he was their **patrōnus**.

An important Roman dressed in his toga. This hot and unwieldy garment was valued because only citizens could wear it.

After seeing these visitors, if he had no further business to conduct at home, Caecilius set out for the **forum** (marketplace), where he spent the rest of the morning trading and banking.

Lunch was eaten at about midday, and it was also a light meal. It usually consisted of some meat or fish followed by fruit. Business ended soon after lunch. Caecilius would then have a short siesta before going to the baths.

Metella would have spent her time directing and supervising the household's many slaves. For example, she might organize a meal and entertainment for her husband and his business friends, as in this Stage.

Bankers in the forum.

Some women also spent time educating their children, especially their daughters, who were less likely than sons to be educated outside the home. In the course of a day, Metella might have enjoyed spending time at home in such activities as reading; but she is just as likely to have gone out to shop or visit friends. She might also have gone to worship at a temple, or visited the baths. On days when a play or a show was put on, she could have attended the theater or amphitheater. Unlike women in Greece or the Near East, Roman women did not have to spend all or most of their time shut away in the home, seldom venturing outside.

Toward the end of the afternoon, the main meal of the day began. This was called **cēna**. During the winter, the family used the inner dining room near the atrium. In the summer, they would generally have preferred the dining room at the back of the house, which looked straight out onto the garden. Three couches were arranged around a circular table which, though small, was very elegantly carved and decorated. Each couch had places for three people. The diners reclined on the couches, leaning on their left elbow and taking food from the table with their right hand. The food was cut up by a slave before being served, and diners ate it with their fingers or a spoon. Forks were not used by the Romans. Not all Romans reclined when eating dinner, but it was usual among rich or upper-class families. Less wealthy people, slaves, children, and sometimes women would eat sitting up.

The meal was not hurried, for this was an occasion for men and women to talk and relax over good food. If guests were invited, some form of entertainment was often provided.

A Roman dinner

The meal began with a first course of light dishes to whet the appetite. Eggs, fish, and cooked and raw vegetables were often served. Then came the main course in which a variety of meat dishes with different sauces and vegetables would be offered. Beef, pork, mutton, and poultry were all popular, and in preparing them the cook would do his best to show off his skill and imagination. Finally, the dessert was brought in, consisting of fruit, nuts, cheese, and sweet dishes. Wine produced locally from the vineyards on Vesuvius was drunk during the meal.

This drawing shows how the couches were arranged in a Roman dining room. The Latin name triclinium means a room with three couches.

The arrows show the position of the people eating dinner.

Many loaves of bread have been found in the ruins of Pompeii.

Roman dinners were said to run "from eggs to apples"; this bowl of eggs has survived from Pompeii.

Fish and other seafood were much enjoyed.

Above and below: *To round off the meal: the fruit bowl and the basket of figs.*

Main course ingredients – a rabbit and a chicken – hanging in a larder.

Vocabulary checklist 2

amīcus	*friend*
ancilla	*slave girl*
cēna	*dinner*
cibus	*food*
dominus	*master*
dormit	*sleeps*
intrat	*enters*
laetus	*happy*
laudat	*praises*
mercātor	*merchant*
quoque	*also*
salūtat	*greets*

Grumio did most of his cooking with pans and grills over charcoal, like a barbecue.

NEGOTIUM

Stage 3

in forō

Caecilius nōn est in vīllā. Caecilius in forō negōtium agit.
Caecilius est argentārius. argentārius pecūniam numerat.

   Caecilius forum circumspectat. ecce! artifex in forō ambulat.
artifex est Clāra. Clāra Caecilium salūtat.

   ecce! tōnsor quoque est in forō. tōnsor est Pantagathus.   5
Caecilius tōnsōrem videt.

     "salvē!" Caecilius tōnsōrem salūtat.

     "salvē!" Pantagathus respondet.

   ecce! vēnālīcius forum intrat. vēnālīcius est Syphāx.
vēnālīcius mercātōrem exspectat. mercātor nōn venit. Syphāx   10
est īrātus. Syphāx mercātōrem vituperat.

in forō *in the forum*

negōtium agit *is working,*
is doing business
ecce! *look!*
artifex *painter, artist*
ambulat *is walking*
tōnsor *barber*

vēnālīcius *slave dealer*
nōn venit *does not come*

artifex

artifex ad vīllam venit. artifex est Clāra. Clāra iānuam pulsat.
Clēmēns artificem nōn audit. servus est in hortō. Clāra clāmat.
canis Clāram audit et lātrat. Quīntus canem audit. Quīntus ad
iānuam venit. fīlius iānuam aperit. Clāra Quīntum salūtat et
vīllam intrat.   5
    Metella est in culīnā. Quīntus mātrem vocat. Metella ātrium
intrat. artifex Metellam salūtat. Metella artificem ad triclīnium
dūcit.
    Clāra in triclīniō labōrat. Clāra pictūram pingit. magnus leō
est in pictūrā. Herculēs quoque est in pictūrā. leō Herculem   10
ferōciter petit. Herculēs magnum fūstem tenet et leōnem
verberat. Herculēs est fortis.
    Caecilius ad vīllam revenit et triclīnium intrat. Caecilius
fīliam vocat. fīlia triclīnium intrat. Lūcia pictūram videt. Lūcia
artificem laudat.   15

ad vīllam	*to the house*
iānuam pulsat	*knocks on the door*
ad iānuam	*to the door*
aperit	*opens*
vocat	*calls*
dūcit	*leads*
pictūram pingit	*paints a picture*
magnus	*big, large*
leō	*lion*
ferōciter	*fiercely*
petit	*is attacking*
fūstem	*club*
tenet	*is holding*
verberat	*is striking*
fortis	*brave, strong*
revenit	*returns*

Roman painters were often very skilled: (left to right) *shepherd boy with pipes; a cupid catching a rabbit; a portrait, possibly of a poet.*

tōnsor

When you have read this story, answer the questions at the end. Answer in English unless you are asked for Latin.

tōnsor in tabernā labōrat. tōnsor est Pantagathus. Caecilius intrat.
    "salvē, tōnsor!" inquit Caecilius.
    "salvē!" respondet Pantagathus.
    tōnsor est occupātus. senex in sellā sedet. Pantagathus
novāculam tenet et barbam tondet. senex novāculam intentē   5
spectat.
    poēta tabernam intrat. poēta in tabernā stat et versum recitat.
versus est scurrīlis. Caecilius rīdet. sed tōnsor nōn rīdet. tōnsor
est īrātus.
    "furcifer! furcifer!" clāmat Pantagathus. senex est perterritus.   10
tōnsor barbam nōn tondet. tōnsor senem secat. multus
sanguis fluit.
    Caecilius surgit et ē tabernā exit.

in tabernā	*in the shop*
inquit	*says*
occupātus	*busy*
senex	*old man*
in sellā	*in the chair*
novāculam	*razor*
barbam tondet	*is trimming his beard*
intentē	*closely, carefully*
poēta	*poet*
versum recitat	*recites a line, recites a verse*
scurrīlis	*rude*
rīdet	*laughs, smiles*
sed	*but*
perterritus	*terrified*
secat	*cuts*
multus	*much*
sanguis	*blood*
fluit	*flows*
ē tabernā	*out of the shop*

Questions

1 Who is working in the shop when Caecilius arrives?
2 **tōnsor est occupātus** (line 4). Look at the rest of the paragraph and say why the barber is described as busy.
3 In line 7, who else comes into the shop?
4 **Caecilius rīdet** (line 8). What makes Caecilius laugh?
5 In lines 8–9, what is the barber's reaction?
6 In line 11, what does the barber do to the old man?
7 What does Caecilius do at the end of the story? Why do you think he does this?
8 Look at the drawing on the right. Which Latin sentence best explains the old man's expression?

vēnālīcius

Caecilius ad portum ambulat. Caecilius portum circumspectat. argentārius nāvem Syriam videt, et ad nāvem ambulat. Syphāx prope nāvem stat.

"salvē, Syphāx!" clāmat argentārius. Syphāx est vēnālīcius. Syphāx Caecilium salūtat. 5

Caecilius servum quaerit. Syphāx rīdet. ecce! Syphāx magnum servum habet. Caecilius servum spectat. argentārius nōn est contentus. argentārius servum nōn emit.

"vīnum!" clāmat Syphāx. ancilla vīnum ad Caecilium portat. argentārius vīnum bibit. 10

Caecilius ancillam spectat. ancilla est pulchra. ancilla rīdet. ancilla Caecilium dēlectat. vēnālīcius quoque rīdet.

"Melissa cēnam optimam coquit," inquit vēnālīcius. "Melissa linguam Latīnam discit. Melissa est docta et pulchra. Melissa …"

"satis! satis!" clāmat Caecilius. Caecilius Melissam emit et ad 15 vīllam revenit. Melissa Grumiōnem dēlectat. Melissa Quīntum dēlectat. ēheu! ancilla Metellam nōn dēlectat.

ad portum	*to the harbor*
nāvem Syriam	*Syrian ship*
prope nāvem	*near the ship*
quaerit	*is looking for*
habet	*has*
contentus	*satisfied*
emit	*buys*
pulchra	*beautiful*
linguam Latīnam	*Latin language*
discit	*is learning*
docta	*skillful, educated*
satis	*enough*
ēheu!	*oh dear! oh no!*

Tools of the trade. A pair of scissors; slave shackles with a padlock (not to same scale).

About the language

1 Remember the difference between the nominative case and accusative case of the following nouns:

nominative	Metella	Caecilius	mercātor
accusative	Metellam	Caecilium	mercātōrem

2 A large number of words, such as **ancilla** and **taberna**, form their accusative case in the same way as **Metella**. They are known as the **first declension**, and look like this:

nominative	Metella	ancilla	taberna
accusative	Metellam	ancillam	tabernam

3 Another large group of nouns is known as the **second declension**. Most of these words form their accusative in the same way as **Caecilius**. For example:

nominative	Caecilius	servus	amīcus
accusative	Caecilium	servum	amīcum

4 You have also met several nouns belonging to the **third declension**. For example:

nominative	mercātor	leō	senex
accusative	mercātōrem	leōnem	senem

The nominative ending of the third declension may take various forms, but the accusative nearly always ends in **-em**.

Pompeian householders loved to have their walls painted with pictures of gardens full of flowers and birds, like this golden oriole.

Practicing the language

1   Write out each sentence, completing it with the correct word from
    the parentheses. Then translate the sentence.

   a   mercātor ē vīllā . . . . (quaerit, ambulat)
   b   servus ad hortum . . . . (recitat, venit)
   c   coquus ad culīnam . . . . (revenit, habet)
   d   artifex ē triclīniō . . . . (laudat, exit)
   e   Syphāx servum ad vīllam . . . . (dūcit, intrat)
   f   Clēmēns cibum ad Caecilium . . . . (clāmat, respondet, portat)

2   Write out each sentence, completing it with the correct case of the
    noun from the parentheses. Then translate the sentence.

   For example: . . . . vīnum portat. (servus, servum)
                 servus vīnum portat.
                 The slave carries the wine.

   a   amīcus . . . . laudat. (servus, servum)
   b   senex . . . . intrat. (taberna, tabernam)
   c   . . . . cibum gustat. (dominus, dominum)
   d   . . . . Metellam salūtat. (mercātor, mercātōrem)
   e   vēnālīcius . . . . videt. (tōnsor, tōnsōrem)
   f   . . . . versum recitat. (poēta, poētam)
   g   . . . . in forō ambulat. (senex, senem)
   h   ancilla . . . . ad ātrium dūcit. (artifex, artificem)

The town of Pompeii

The town of Pompeii was built on a low hill of volcanic
rock about five miles (eight kilometers) south of
Mount Vesuvius and close to the mouth of a small
river. It was one of a number of prosperous towns in
the fertile region of Campania. Outside the towns,
especially along the coast of the bay, there were many
villas and farming estates, often owned by wealthy
Romans who were attracted to the area by its pleasant
climate and peaceful surroundings.

Villas along the bay.

The town itself covered 163 acres (66 hectares), and was surrounded by a wall. The wall had eleven towers and eight gates. Roads led out from these gates to the neighboring towns of Herculaneum, Nola, Nuceria, Stabiae, and to the harbor.

Two wide main streets, known nowadays as the Street of Shops and Stabiae Street, crossed near the center of the town. A third main street ran parallel to the Street of Shops. The other streets, most of which also ran in straight lines, divided the town neatly into blocks. Most streets probably did not have names, and a stranger visiting the town would have had to ask the way from the local people. The present names were invented in modern times to make it easier to identify the streets. The streets, constructed of volcanic stone, had high paved sidewalks on one or both sides to enable pedestrians to avoid the traffic of wagons, horses, and mules, and to keep clear of the rubbish and rainwater that collected in the roadway. Stepping-stones provided convenient crossing places.

A street in Pompeii in the rain.

Below: *Buildings around the forum:*
1 *Temple of Jupiter;* 2 *Market;* 3 *Temples of the Emperors and the Lares of Pompeii;* 4 *Eumachia's building;* 5 *Polling station;* 6 *Municipal offices;* 7 *Basilica;* 8 *Temple of Apollo;* 9 *Vegetable market and public lavatory.*

Pompeii

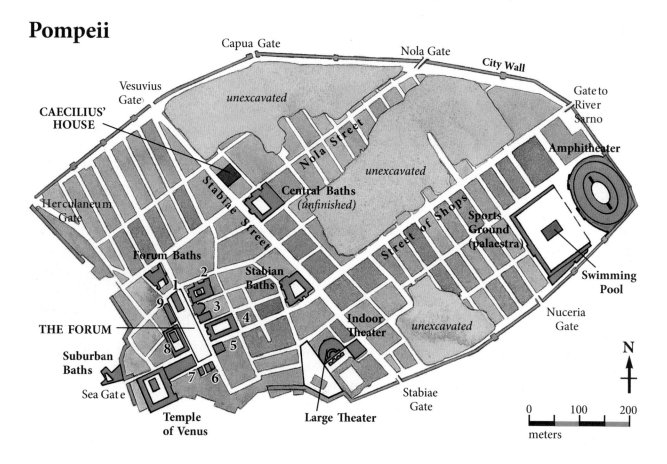

The town's water supply was brought from the hills by an aqueduct; on reaching Pompeii it was stored in large tanks on high ground at the northern side. The pressure created by the water in these tanks provided a good flow through underground lead pipes to all parts of the town, including the three sets of public baths. Public fountains, like this one in the Street of Shops, stood at many street corners. Most people drew their water from these, but wealthier citizens paid special rates so that they could take a private supply straight into their homes.

In all the main streets there were bakers' shops and bars where hot and cold drinks and snacks could be bought. The main shopping areas were in the forum and along the Street of Shops to the northeast of the Stabian Baths. Carved or painted signs indicated different kinds of store: the figure of a goat announced a dairy; a hammer and chisel advertised a stonemason. General advertisements and public notices were painted on the whitewashed walls outside shops and houses. We can still see notices advertising shows in the amphitheater, and political slogans supporting candidates in the local elections.

At the western end of the town was the forum. This large and impressive open space, with a covered colonnade on three sides, was the center for business, local government, and religion.

A bakery. On the left are two corn mills, worked by slaves or donkeys, and at the back is the bread oven.

There were two theaters. Popular shows for large audiences were performed in the big open-air theater, which could hold about 5,000 people, while the smaller one, which was roofed, was used for concerts and for other shows. At the eastern end of the town was a huge sports ground or **palaestra**, and next to it an amphitheater in which gladiatorial combats and wild-animal hunts were staged. This amphitheater was large enough to seat every inhabitant in Pompeii and visitors from neighboring towns as well.

Like a modern seaport, Pompeii was a place where people of many nationalities were to be seen: Romans, Greeks, Syrians, Jews, Africans, Spaniards, and probably several other nationalities as well, with their different languages and different religions. This regular coming and going of people, many of whom were merchants and businessmen, was made possible by the peaceful conditions that existed throughout the provinces of the Roman empire at this time.

From Britain in the northwest to Syria and Palestine in the east, Rome maintained peace and provided firm government. The frontiers of the empire were held secure by Roman troops stationed at important points. A system of well-built roads made travel by land relatively easy and provided an effective means of communication between Rome and distant parts of the empire. For many purposes, particularly for trade, travel by sea was more convenient. Ships carried cargoes of building materials, foodstuffs, and luxury goods across the Mediterranean; taxes were collected in the provinces and the wealth of Rome increased. Pompeii was not a large town, but played its part in the flourishing life of the empire.

Stabiae Street today.

Streets of Pompeii

Set against a background of a piece of painted wall, here are some glimpses of the streets of Pompeii.

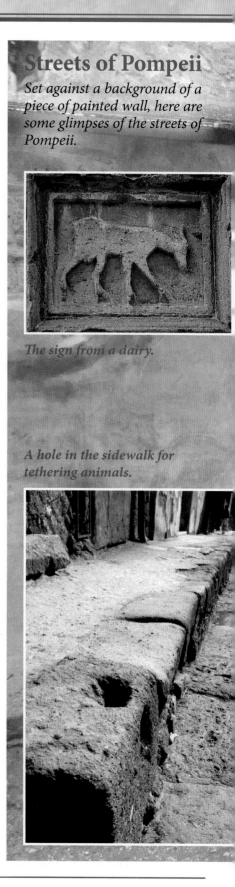

The sign from a dairy.

A hole in the sidewalk for tethering animals.

A plaster cast of shop shutters.

A house with its second story overhanging the road to gain a little extra floor space; often the second floor was a separate apartment. (The street signs are modern.)

A section of wall covered with painted slogans.

Counters and wine storage jars (amphorae) are still in place in some of the bars and food shops (right). Some also have paintings on the walls inside which show the customers drinking and gambling (above).

Vocabulary checklist 3

ad	*to*
bibit	*drinks*
circumspectat	*looks around*
clāmat	*shouts*
ecce!	*look!*
et	*and*
exit	*goes out*
exspectat	*waits for*
iānua	*door*
īrātus	*angry*
leō	*lion*
magnus	*big, large, great*
nāvis	*ship*
nōn	*not*
portat	*carries*
respondet	*replies*
rīdet	*laughs, smiles*
salvē!	*hello!*
surgit	*gets up, stands up*
taberna	*store, shop, inn*
videt	*sees*
vīnum	*wine*

This painting shows Mercury, the god of profit as well as the messenger of the gods. It is painted above a cloth workshop in the Street of Shops, to bring success to the business.

IN FORO

Stage 4

1 Grumiō: ego sum coquus.
         ego cēnam coquō.

2 Caecilius: ego sum argentārius.
            ego pecūniam habeō.

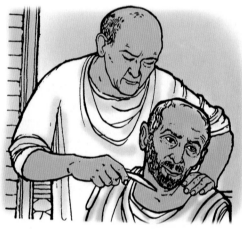

3 Pantagathus: ego sum tōnsor.
                ego barbam tondeō.

4 Syphāx: ego sum vēnālīcius.
            ego servum vēndō.

5 poēta: ego sum poēta.
           ego versum recitō.

6 Clāra: ego sum artifex.
           ego leōnem pingō.

7 Quīntus: quid tū coquis?
Grumiō: ego cēnam coquō.

8 Lūcia: quid tū habēs?
Caecilius: ego pecūniam habeō.

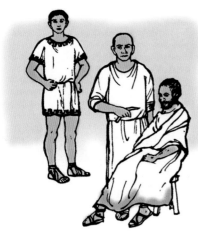

9 Quīntus: quid tū tondēs?
tōnsor: ego barbam tondeō.

10 Lūcia: quid tū vēndis?
vēnālīcius: ego servum vēndō.

11 Quīntus: quid tū recitās?
poēta: ego versum recitō.

12 Lūcia: quid tū pingis?
artifex: ego leōnem pingō.

13 Metella: quis es tū?
   ancilla: ego sum Melissa.

14 Metella: quis es tū?
   vēnālīcius: ego sum Syphāx.

15 Metella: quis es tū?
   tōnsor: ego sum Pantagathus.

A corner of the forum, with shops opening off a colonnade.

Hermogenēs

Caecilius est in forō. Caecilius in forō argentāriam habet.
Hermogenēs ad forum venit. Hermogenēs est mercātor Graecus.
mercātor nāvem habet. mercātor Caecilium salūtat.

    "ego sum mercātor Graecus," inquit Hermogenēs. "ego sum
mercātor probus. ego pecūniam quaerō."   5

    "cūr tū pecūniam quaeris?" inquit Caecilius. "tū nāvem habēs."

    "sed nāvis nōn adest," respondet Hermogenēs. "nāvis est in
Graeciā. ego pecūniam nōn habeō. ego tamen sum probus. ego
semper pecūniam reddō."

    "ecce!" inquit Caecilius. "ego cēram habeō. tū ānulum habēs?"   10

    "ego ānulum habeō," respondet Hermogenēs. "ānulus signum
habet. ecce! ego signum in cērā imprimō."

    Caecilius pecūniam trādit. mercātor pecūniam capit et ē forō
currit.

    ēheu! Hermogenēs nōn revenit. mercātor pecūniam nōn   15
reddit. Caecilius Hermogenem ad basilicam vocat.

argentāriam *banker's
         stall*
Graecus *Greek*
probus *honest*
cūr? *why?*
nōn adest *is not here*
in Graeciā *in Greece*
tamen *however*
semper *always*
ego reddō *I give back*
cēram *wax tablet*
ānulum *ring*
signum *seal, sign*
ego imprimō *I press*
trādit *hands over*
capit *takes*
currit *runs*
ad basilicam *to the law
         court*

in basilicā

iūdex basilicam intrat.

iūdex:	quis es tū?	
Caecilius:	ego sum Lūcius Caecilius Iūcundus.	
iūdex:	tū es Pompēiānus?	
Caecilius:	ego sum Pompēiānus.	5
iūdex:	quid tū in urbe agis?	
Caecilius:	ego cotīdiē ad forum veniō. ego sum argentārius.	
iūdex:	cūr tū hodiē ad basilicam venīs?	
Caecilius:	Hermogenēs multam pecūniam dēbet. Hermogenēs pecūniam nōn reddit.	10
Hermogenēs:	Caecilius est mendāx!	
iūdex:	quis es tū?	
Hermogenēs:	ego sum Hermogenēs.	
iūdex:	Hermogenēs, quid tū in urbe agis?	15
Hermogenēs:	ego in forō negōtium agō. ego sum mercātor.	
iūdex:	quid tū respondēs? tū pecūniam dēbēs?	
Hermogenēs:	ego pecūniam nōn dēbeō. amīcus meus est testis.	
amīcus:	ego sum testis. Hermogenēs pecūniam nōn dēbet. Caecilius est mendāx.	20
Caecilius:	tū, Hermogenēs, es mendāx. amīcus tuus quoque est mendāx. tū pecūniam nōn reddis …	
iūdex:	satis! tū Hermogenem accūsās, sed tū rem nōn probās.	25
Caecilius:	ego cēram habeō. tū signum in cērā vidēs.	
Hermogenēs:	ēheu!	
iūdex:	Hermogenēs, tū ānulum habēs?	
Caecilius:	ecce! Hermogenēs ānulum cēlat.	
iūdex:	ubi est ānulus? ecce! ānulus rem probat. ego Hermogenem convincō.	30

iūdex *judge*

quis? *who?*

Pompēiānus *a citizen of Pompeii, Pompeian*

quid tū agis? *what do you do?*
in urbe *in the city*
cotīdiē *every day*
hodiē *today*
dēbet *owes*

mendāx *liar*

meus *my*
testis *witness*

tuus *your*

tū accūsās *you accuse*
tū rem nōn probās *you do not prove the case*

cēlat *is hiding*
ubi? *where?*
ego convincō *I convict, I find guilty*

Some sealstones from rings and a gold seal ring without a stone. The stone on the left is enlarged.

About the language

1 In the first three Stages, you met sentences like this:

ancilla ambulat.   mercātor sedet.   servus currit.

The slave girl walks.   *The merchant sits.*   *The slave runs.*

All of these sentences have a noun (**ancilla**, **mercātor**, **servus**) and a word indicating the action of the sentence, known as the **verb**. In the sentences above the verbs are **ambulat**, **sedet**, **currit**.

In all the sentences you met in the first three Stages, the verb ended in **-t**.

2 In Stage 4, you have met sentences with **ego** and **tū**:

ego ambulō. *I walk.*   **ego** sedeō. *I sit.*   **ego** currō. *I run.*

tū ambulās. *You walk.*   **tū** sedēs. *You sit.*   **tū** curris. *You run.*

3 Notice the three different forms of each word:

ego ambul**ō**.   ego sede**ō**.   ego curr**ō**.

tū ambulā**s**.   tū sedē**s**.   tū curri**s**.

ancilla ambula**t**.   mercātor sede**t**.   servus curri**t**.

Notice also that the words **ego** and **tū** are not strictly necessary, since the endings **-ō** and **-s** make it clear that "I" and "you" are performing the action of the sentence. The Romans generally used **ego** and **tū** for emphasis.

4 The following example is rather different:

ego **sum** īrātus.   tū **es** īrātus.   servus **est** īrātus.

I am angry.   *You are angry.*   *The slave is angry.*

5 Further examples:

a Caecilius recitat. ego recitō.

b Quīntus dormit. tū dormīs.

c tū labōrās. servus labōrat.

d Syphāx servum habet. ego servum habeō.

e ego pecūniam trādō. tū pecūniam trādis.

f Pantagathus est tōnsor. tū es mercātor. ego sum poēta.

g ambulō; circumspectō; circumspectās; es.

h sum; audiō; audīs; habēs.

1 Write out each pair of sentences, completing the second sentence
with the correct verb from the parentheses. Translate both sentences.

a   ego sum coquus.
    ego cēnam .... (dormiō, coquō)
b   ego sum mercātor.
    ego nāvem .... (stō, habeō)
c   ego sum Herculēs.
    ego fūstem .... (teneō, sedeō)
d   ego sum servus.
    ego in culīnā .... (habeō, labōrō)
e   tū es amīcus.
    tū vīllam .... (intrās, dūcis)
f   tū es ancilla.
    tū suāviter .... (venīs, cantās)
g   tū es mendāx.
    tū pecūniam .... (dēbēs, ambulās)
h   tū es iūdex.
    tū Hermogenem .... (curris, convincis)
i   ego sum Syphāx.
    ego ancillam .... (vēndō, ambulō)
j   tū es senex.
    tū in tabernā .... (tenēs, sedēs)

*The basilica (law court)
was a large, long building
with rows of pillars inside
and a high platform at
the far end on which the
town's senior officials
may have sat when
hearing lawsuits.*

2 Translate this story:

Grumiō et leō

Clāra in vīllā labōrat. Clāra pictūram in triclīniō pingit. magnus leō est in pictūrā. Clāra ē vīllā discēdit.

    Grumiō ē tabernā revenit et vīllam intrat. Grumiō est ēbrius. Grumiō pictūram videt. Grumiō est perterritus.

    "ēheu!" inquit Grumiō. "leō est in triclīniō. leō mē spectat. leō mē ferōciter petit."   5

    Grumiō ē triclīniō currit et culīnam intrat. Clēmēns est in culīnā. Clēmēns Grumiōnem spectat.

    "cūr tū es perterritus?" inquit Clēmēns.

    "ēheu! leō est in triclīniō," inquit Grumiō.   10

    "ita vērō," respondet Clēmēns, "et servus ēbrius est in culīnā."

discēdit departs, leaves
ē tabernā from the inn
ēbrius drunk

mē me

ita vērō yes

This comic painting comes from Pompeii and shows a Roman-style trial taking place before a judge and his two advisers, with soldiers to keep order.

One of Caecilius' tablets, with a special groove in the center to hold wax seals.

The forum

The forum was the heart of the commercial, administrative, and religious life of Pompeii. It was a large open space surrounded on three sides by a colonnade, with various important buildings grouped closely round it. The open area, 156 yards (143 meters) long and 42 yards (38 meters) wide, was paved with stone. In it stood a number of statues commemorating the emperor, members of the emperor's family, and local citizens who had given distinguished service to the town.

The drawing below shows a typical scene in the forum. The trader on the left has set up his wooden stall and is selling small articles of ironware, pincers, knives, and hammers; the trader on the right is a shoemaker. He has seated his customers on stools while he shows them his goods. Behind the traders is the colonnade. This elegant structure, supported by columns of white marble, provided an open corridor in which people could walk and do business out of the heat of the sun in summer and out of the rain in winter.

Some women took part in commerce and trade. Although it was unusual for women to manage their own businesses, widows occasionally took over control of their husbands' business affairs. One influential Pompeian woman was Eumachia (right), a priestess and a patroness of the powerful clothworkers. She inherited money from her father and paid for a large building which may have been a market, perhaps for cloth traders. Among less wealthy women, we hear of those who worked as cooks, bakers, weavers, hairdressers, shoemakers, silversmiths, midwives, and doctors.

In the drawing below are two statues of important citizens mounted on horseback. Behind them is one of the bronze gates through which people entered the forum. The whole forum

Part of the colonnade, which had two stories, seen from inside. You can see the holes for the floor beams of the top story.

Drawing based on a Pompeian wall painting. Another scene from the same painting can be seen opposite.

Eumachia, a priestess and wealthy Pompeian patroness of the clothworkers.

area was for pedestrians only and a row of upright stones at each entrance provided an effective barrier to wheeled traffic. You can see two of these stones in the picture on page 39.

In the Pompeian wall painting below, you see a public bulletin board fixed across the pedestals of three statues, and people studying the notices. There were no newspapers in Pompeii, but certain kinds of information, such as election results and dates of processions and shows, had to be publicized. This was done by putting up bulletin boards in the forum.

In addition to official announcements, a large number of graffiti have been found in the forum and elsewhere, in which ordinary citizens recorded lost property, announced accommodation to let, left lovers' messages, and publicized the problems they were having with their neighbors. One example reads:

A bronze jar has been lost from this shop.
A reward is offered for its recovery.

Another complains of noise at night and asks the **aedile** (the official who was responsible for law and order) to do something about it:

Macerior requests the aedile to stop people from making a noise in the streets and disturbing decent folk who are asleep.

This statue of a distinguished citizen on horseback was found in nearby Herculaneum, but is very similar to the left-hand statue in the Pompeian painting on the left.

Reading the bulletin boards.

Some of the most important public buildings were situated around the forum. In a prominent position at the north end stood the temple of Jupiter, the greatest of the Roman gods (see 1 opposite). It was probably from the steps of this temple that political speeches were made at election times.

Next to the temple was a large covered market (2) which contained permanent shops rather than temporary stalls. The traders here sold mainly meat, fish, and vegetables. A public weights and measures table (10) ensured that they gave fair measures.

Immediately to the south of the market was a temple dedicated to the **Larēs**, the guardian spirits of Pompeii (3), and next to that stood a temple in honor of the Roman emperors (4). Across the forum was the temple of Apollo (9), and near the southwest corner of the forum was the temple of Venus, an important goddess for the Pompeians, who believed that she took a special interest in their town.

We have now mentioned five religious shrines around or near the forum. There were many others elsewhere in the town, including a temple of Isis, an Egyptian goddess, whose worship had been brought to Italy. In addition to these public shrines, each home had its own small shrine, the lararium, where the family's own Lares, who looked after their household, were worshipped. The Pompeians believed in many gods, rather than one, and it seemed to them quite natural to believe that different gods should care for different parts of human life. Apollo, for example, was associated with law, medicine, and music; Venus was the goddess of love and beauty.

In a prominent site on the east side of the forum was a large building which may have been a market, perhaps for cloth traders (5). It was built with money given by Eumachia. Next to it was the polling station, an open hall used for voting in elections (6), and along the south side were three municipal offices (7), whose exact purpose is not known. They may have been the treasury, the record office, and the meeting room of the town council.

At the southwest corner stood the **basilica**, or law court (8). The basilica was also used as a meeting place for businessmen.

Forum – focus of life

Business, religion, local government: these were the official purposes of the forum and its surrounding buildings. This great crowded square was the center of much of the open-air life in Pompeii. Here people gathered to do business, to shop, or to meet friends. Strangers visiting the forum would have been struck by its size, the splendid buildings surrounding it, and the general air of prosperity.

Carving from Eumachia's building.

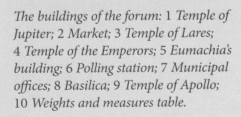

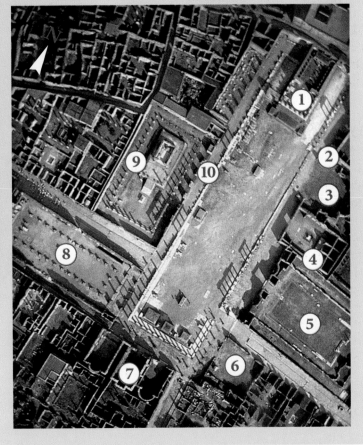

The buildings of the forum: 1 *Temple of Jupiter*; 2 *Market*; 3 *Temple of Lares*; 4 *Temple of the Emperors*; 5 *Eumachia's building*; 6 *Polling station*; 7 *Municipal offices*; 8 *Basilica*; 9 *Temple of Apollo*; 10 *Weights and measures table*.

Vocabulary checklist 4

agit	does
ānulus	ring
coquit	cooks
cūr?	why?
ē	from, out of
ego	I
ēheu!	oh dear! oh no!
habet	has
inquit	says
iūdex	judge
mendāx	liar
pecūnia	money
perterritus	terrified
poēta	poet
quaerit	looks for, searches for
quis?	who?
reddit	gives back
satis	enough
sed	but
signum	sign, seal
tū	you
vocat	calls

This marble carving was found in Caecilius' house. It shows the temple of Jupiter with statues of men on horseback on each side, as it looked during an earthquake that happened in AD 62 or 63.

IN THEATRO

Stage 5

in viā

1 canis est in viā.

2 canēs sunt in viā.

3 servus est in viā.

4 servī sunt in viā.

5   puella est in viā.

6   puellae sunt in viā.

7   puer est in viā.

8   puerī sunt in viā.

9   mercātor est in viā.

10 mercātōrēs sunt in viā.

in theātrō

11 spectātor in theātrō sedet.

12 spectātōrēs in theātrō sedent.

13 āctor in scaenā stat.

14 āctōrēs in scaenā stant.

15 fēmina spectat.

16 fēminae spectant.

17 senex dormit.

18 senēs dormiunt.

19 iuvenis plaudit.

20 iuvenēs plaudunt.

āctōrēs

magna turba est in urbe. fēminae et puellae sunt in turbā. senēs
quoque et iuvenēs sunt in turbā. servī hodiē nōn labōrant. senēs
hodiē nōn dormiunt. mercātōrēs hodiē nōn sunt occupātī.
Pompēiānī sunt ōtiōsī. urbs tamen nōn est quiēta. Pompēiānī ad
theātrum contendunt. magnus clāmor est in urbe.   5

   agricolae urbem intrant. nautae urbem petunt. pāstōrēs dē
monte veniunt et ad urbem contendunt. turba per portam ruit.

   nūntius in forō clāmat: "āctōrēs sunt in urbe. āctōrēs sunt in
theātrō. Priscus fābulam dat. Priscus fābulam optimam dat.
āctōrēs sunt Actius et Sorex."   10

   Caecilius et Metella ē vīllā discēdunt. argentārius et uxor ad
theātrum ambulant. Quīntus et Lūcia ad theātrum contendunt.
Clēmēns et Melissa ad theātrum currunt. sed Grumiō in vīllā
manet.

āctōrēs *actors*

turba *crowd*
fēminae *women*
puellae *girls*
iuvenēs *young men*
ōtiōsī *on holiday, idle,
    taking time off*
quiēta *quiet*
ad theātrum *to the theater*
contendunt *hurry*
clāmor *shout, uproar*
agricolae *farmers*
nautae *sailors*
petunt *head for*
pāstōrēs *shepherds*
dē monte *down from the
    mountain*
per portam ruit *rushes
    through the gate*
nūntius *messenger*
fābulam dat *is putting on
    a play*
uxor *wife*
manet *remains, stays*

*Two actors in mask and
costume. These statues were
found in the garden of a
house in Pompeii.*

About the language 1

1   In the first four Stages, you have met sentences like these:

>   puella sedet.   servus labōrat.
>   *The girl is sitting.*   *The slave is working.*
>
>   leō currit.   mercātor dormit.
>   *The lion is running.*   *The merchant is sleeping.*

Sentences like these refer to **one** person or thing, and in each sentence the form of both words (the noun and the verb) is said to be **singular**.

2   Sentences which refer to **more than one** person or thing use a different form of the words, known as the **plural**. Compare the singular and plural forms in the following sentences:

>   *singular*   *plural*
>   puella labōrat.   puellae labōrant.
>   *The girl is working.*   *The girls are working.*
>
>   servus rīdet.   servī rīdent.
>   *The slave is laughing.*   *The slaves are laughing.*
>
>   leō currit.   leōnēs currunt.
>   *The lion is running.*   *The lions are running.*
>
>   mercātor dormit.   mercātōrēs dormiunt.
>   *The merchant is sleeping.*   *The merchants are sleeping.*

Note that in each of these sentences **both** the noun and the verb show the difference between singular and plural.

3   Look again at the sentences in paragraph 2 and note the difference between the singular and plural forms of the verb.

>   *singular*   *plural*
>   labōrat   labōrant
>   rīdet   rīdent
>   currit   currunt
>   dormit   dormiunt

In each case the singular ending is **-t** and the plural ending is **-nt**.

4 Notice how Latin shows the difference between "is" and "are":

mercātor **est** in viā.　　　　　mercātōrēs **sunt** in viā.
The merchant is in the street.　*The merchants are in the street.*

*Fragment of wall painting showing an actor
in the dressing room, studying his mask.*

Poppaea

Poppaea est ancilla. ancilla prope iānuam stat. ancilla viam spectat.
dominus in hortō dormit. dominus est Lucriō. Lucriō est senex.

Poppaea:	ego amīcum meum exspectō. ubi est amīcus?	
	(Lucriō stertit.)	
	ēheu! Lucriō est in vīllā.	5
	(agricolae in viā clāmant.)	
agricolae:	euge! agricolae hodiē nōn labōrant!	**euge!** *hurray!*
Poppaea:	Lucriō! Lucriō! agricolae urbem intrant.	
	agricolae adsunt.	**adsunt** *are here*
Lucriō:	*(sēmisomnus)* a...a...agricolae?	10 **sēmisomnus** *half-asleep*
puerī:	euge! Sorex! Actius! āctōrēs adsunt.	
Poppaea:	Lucriō! Lucriō! puerī per viam currunt.	**puerī** *boys*
Lucriō:	quid tū clāmās, Poppaea? cūr tū clāmōrem facis?	**tū clāmōrem facis** *you are*
Poppaea:	Lucriō, Pompēiānī clāmōrem faciunt.	*making a noise*
	agricolae et puerī sunt in viā.	15
Lucriō:	cūr tū mē vexās?	**tū vexās** *you annoy*
Poppaea:	āctōrēs in theātrō fābulam agunt.	**fābulam agunt** *act in a play*
Lucriō:	āctōrēs?	
Poppaea:	Sorex et Actius adsunt.	
Lucriō:	quid tū dīcis?	20 **tū dīcis** *you say*
Poppaea:	*(īrāta)* senēs ad theātrum ambulant, iuvenēs	
	ad theātrum contendunt, omnēs Pompēiānī	**omnēs** *all*
	ad theātrum ruunt. āctōrēs in theātrō fābulam agunt.	**ruunt** *rush*
Lucriō:	euge! āctōrēs adsunt. ego quoque ad theātrum	
	contendō.	25
	(exit Lucriō. amīcus vīllam intrat.)	
amīcus:	salvē! mea columba!	**mea columba** *my dove, my*
Poppaea:	Grumiō, dēliciae meae! salvē!	*dear*
Grumiō:	ubi est dominus tuus?	**dēliciae meae** *my darling*
Poppaea:	Lucriō abest.	30 **abest** *is out*
Grumiō:	euge!	

1 Study the following examples of singular and plural forms:

singular	*plural*
puella rīdet.	**puellae** rīdent.
The girl is smiling.	*The girls are smiling.*
servus ambulat.	**servī** ambulant.
The slave is walking.	*The slaves are walking.*
mercātor contendit.	**mercātōrēs** contendunt.
The merchant is hurrying.	*The merchants are hurrying.*

2 Each of the nouns in **boldface** is in the nominative case, because it refers to a person or persons who are performing some action, such as walking or smiling.

3 **puella**, **servus**, and **mercātor** are therefore **nominative singular**, and **puellae**, **servī**, and **mercātōrēs** are **nominative plural**.

4 Notice the forms of the nominative plural in the different declensions:

first declension	*second declension*	*third declension*
puellae	servī	mercātōrēs
ancillae	amīcī	leōnēs
fēminae	puerī	senēs

5 Further examples:

a amīcus ambulat. amīcī ambulant.
b āctor clāmat. āctōrēs clāmant.
c fēminae plaudunt. fēmina plaudit.
d vēnālīciī intrant. vēnālīcius intrat.
e ancilla respondet. ancillae respondent.
f senēs dormiunt. senex dormit.

6 Examples with **est** and **sunt**:

a spectātor est in theātrō. spectātōrēs sunt in theātrō.
b fēminae sunt in forō. fēmina est in forō.
c amīcī sunt in triclīniō. amīcus est in triclīniō.
d agricola adest. agricolae adsunt.

Practicing the language

1 Write out each sentence, completing it with the correct form of the verb from the parentheses. Then translate the sentence.

> For example: senēs . . . . (dormit, dormiunt)
> senēs **dormiunt**.
> *The old men are sleeping.*

a senēs in forō . . . . (dormit, dormiunt)
b puellae in theātrō . . . . (sedent, sedet)
c agricolae ad urbem . . . . (currunt, currit)
d Pompēiānī clāmōrem . . . . (facit, faciunt)
e servī ad theātrum . . . . (contendit, contendunt)

2 Write out each sentence, completing it with the correct form of the verb from the parentheses. Then translate the sentence.

a pāstōrēs ad theātrum . . . . (contendit, contendunt)
b pāstor pecūniam nōn . . . . (habet, habent)
c puella āctōrem . . . . (laudat, laudant)
d fēminae fābulam . . . . (spectat, spectant)
e vēnālīciī ad urbem . . . . (venit, veniunt)
f nūntius in forō . . . . (clāmat, clāmant)
g āctōrēs . . . . (adest, adsunt)
h pater . . . . in tablīnō. (est, sunt)

3 Translate this story:

in theātrō

hodiē Pompēiānī sunt ōtiōsī. dominī et servī nōn
labōrant. multī Pompēiānī in theātrō sedent.
spectātōrēs Actium exspectant. tandem Actius in
scaenā stat. Pompēiānī plaudunt.

    subitō Pompēiānī magnum clāmōrem audiunt.   5
servus theātrum intrat. "euge! fūnambulus adest,"
clāmat servus. Pompēiānī Actium nōn spectant. omnēs
Pompēiānī ē theātrō currunt et fūnambulum spectant.

    nēmō in theātrō manet. Actius tamen nōn est īrātus.
Actius quoque fūnambulum spectat.   10

multī *many*
spectātōrēs *spectators*
tandem *at last*
in scaenā *on the stage*
plaudunt *applaud, clap*
subitō *suddenly*
fūnambulus *tightrope*
    walker
nēmō *no one*

The theater at Pompeii

Plays were not performed in Pompeii every day but only at festivals, which were held several times a year. There was therefore all the more excitement in the town when the notices appeared announcing a performance. On the day itself the shops were closed and no business was done in the forum. Men and women with their slaves set off for the theater early in the morning. Some carried cushions, because the seats were made of stone, and many took food and drink for the day. The only people who did not need to hurry were the town councillors and other important citizens, for whom the best seats at the front of the auditorium were reserved. These important people carried tokens which indicated the entrance they should use and where they were to sit. It is uncertain whether men and women sat separately or together, and women may have had to be content with a seat at the top of the large semicircular auditorium. The large theater at Pompeii could hold 5,000 people.

A dramatic performance was a public occasion, and admission to the theater was free. All the expenses were paid by a wealthy citizen, who provided the actors, the producer, the scenery, and costumes. He volunteered to do this, not only to benefit his fellow-citizens, but also to gain popularity which would be useful in local political elections.

A bronze head of Sorex, a famous Pompeian actor. Originally the eyes would have been inserted in lifelike colors.

Pompeii's smaller, roofed theater.

Pompeii's main, open-air theater.

The performance consisted of a series of plays and lasted all day, even during the heat of the afternoon. To keep the spectators cool, a large awning was suspended by ropes and pulleys across most of the theater. The awning was managed by sailors, who were used to handling ropes and canvas; even so, on a windy day the awning could not be unfurled, and the audience had to make use of hats or sunshades to protect themselves from the sun. Between plays, scented water was sprinkled by attendants.

One of the most popular kinds of production was the **pantomime**, a mixture of opera and ballet. The plot, which was usually serious, was taken from the Greek myths. The parts of the different characters were mimed and danced by one masked performer, while a chorus sang the lyrics. An orchestra containing such instruments as the lyre, double pipes, trumpet, and castanets accompanied the performance, providing a rhythmical beat. Although there is evidence that women and girls sometimes performed in pantomimes, most performers were men who were usually Greek slaves or freedmen. They were much admired for their skill and stamina, and attracted a large following of fans.

Equally popular were the comic actors. The bronze statue of one of these, Sorex, was discovered at Pompeii, together with graffiti on walls naming other popular actors. One of these reads:

Actius, our favorite, come back quickly.

A mosaic of a theater musician.

A clay model of a mask, perhaps for the character Manducus.

The comedies of Plautus

There is usually a young man from a respectable family who is leading a wild life; he is often in debt and in love with a pretty but unsuitable slave girl. His father, who is old-fashioned and disapproving, has to be kept in the dark by deception. The son is usually helped in this by a cunning slave, who gets himself and his young master in and out of trouble at great speed. Eventually it is discovered that the girl is freeborn and from a good family. The young man is therefore able to marry his true love and all ends happily.

Comic actors were always male. They appeared in vulgar farces which were often put on at the end of longer performances. These short plays were about Italian country life and were packed with rude jokes and slapstick. They used just a few familiar characters, such as Pappus, an old fool, and Manducus, a greedy clown. These characters were instantly recognizable from the strange masks worn by the actors. The Roman poet, Juvenal, describes a performance of a play of this kind in a country theater, where the children sitting on their mothers' laps shrank back in horror when they saw the gaping, white masks. These masks, like those used in other plays, were probably made of linen which was covered with plaster and painted.

Sometimes, at a festival, the comedies of Plautus and Terence may have been put on. These plays also used a number of familiar characters, but the plots were complicated and the dialogue more witty than that of the farces.

2 The boy has been with his beloved slave girl (here's her mask).

1 Father has to be restrained from violence when he finds his son coming home drunk from a party. The cunning slave props the lad up. A musician is playing the double pipes.

3 The slave sits on an altar for sanctuary, hoping to escape terrible punishment.

4 The slave uncovers a basket in the girl's possession and finds her baby clothes – they are recognized! She must be the long-lost daughter of father's best friend and wrongly enslaved by pirates! All live happily ever after.

Vocabulary checklist 5

adest	*is here*
adsunt	*are here*
agricola	*farmer*
ambulat	*walks*
audit	*hears, listens to*
clāmor	*shout, uproar*
contendit	*hurries*
currit	*runs*
fābula	*play, story*
fēmina	*woman*
hodiē	*today*
iuvenis	*young man*
meus	*my, mine*
multus	*much*
multī	*many*
optimus	*very good, excellent, best*
petit	*heads for, attacks*
plaudit	*applauds, claps*
puella	*girl*
senex	*old man*
spectat	*looks at, watches*
stat	*stands*
turba	*crowd*
ubi?	*where?*
urbs	*city*
venit	*comes*

This tightrope walker from a wall painting is a satyr, one of the followers of Bacchus, god of wine. He has a tail and plays the double pipes.

FELIX

Stage 6

1   servī per viam ambulābant.

2   canis subitō lātrāvit.

3   Grumiō canem timēbat.

4   "pestis!" clāmāvit coquus.

5   Clēmēns erat fortis.

6   sed canis Clēmentem superāvit.

7   Quīntus per viam ambulābat.

8   iuvenis clāmōrem audīvit.

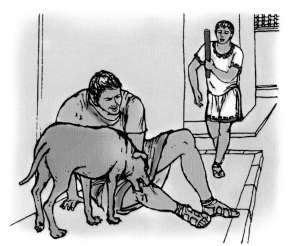

9   canis Clēmentem vexābat.

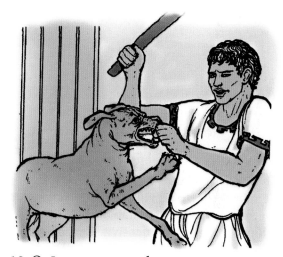

10 Quīntus canem pulsāvit.

11 servī erant laetī.

12 servī Quīntum laudāvērunt.

pugna

Clēmēns in forō ambulābat. turba maxima erat in forō. servī et ancillae cibum emēbant. multī pistōrēs pānem vēndēbant. poēta recitābat. mercātor Graecus contentiōnem cum agricolā habēbat. mercātor īrātus pecūniam postulābat. subitō agricola Graecum pulsāvit, quod Graecus agricolam vituperābat. Pompēiānī rīdēbant, et agricolam incitābant. Clēmēns, postquam clāmōrem audīvit, ad pugnam festīnāvit. tandem agricola mercātōrem superāvit et ē forō agitāvit. Pompēiānī agricolam fortem laudāvērunt.

pugna *fight*

maxima *very large*
erat *was*
pistōrēs *bakers*
pānem vēndēbant
    were selling bread
contentiōnem habēbat
  was having an argument
cum agricolā *with a farmer*
postulābat *was demanding*
pulsāvit *hit, punched*
quod *because*
incitābant *were urging on*
postquam *when, after*
festīnāvit *hurried*
superāvit *overpowered*
agitāvit *chased*

5

Fēlīx

multī Pompēiānī in tabernā vīnum bibēbant. Clēmēns tabernam intrāvit. subitō Clēmēns "Fēlīx!" clāmāvit. Clēmēns Fēlīcem laetē salūtāvit. Fēlīx erat lībertus.

Clēmēns Fēlīcem ad vīllam invītāvit. Clēmēns et Fēlīx vīllam intrāvērunt. Lūcia in ātriō stābat. Fēlīx Lūciam salūtāvit. Clēmēns Caecilium et Metellam quaesīvit. Caecilius in hortō legēbat. Metella in tablīnō scrībēbat. Caecilius et Metella ad ātrium festīnāvērunt et Fēlīcem salūtāvērunt. postquam Quīntus ātrium intrāvit, Fēlīx iuvenem spectāvit. lībertus erat valdē commōtus. paene lacrimābat; sed rīdēbat.

tum Clēmēns ad culīnam festīnāvit. Grumiō in culīnā dormiēbat. Clēmēns coquum excitāvit et tōtam rem nārrāvit. coquus, quod erat laetus, cēnam optimam parāvit.

laetē *happily*
lībertus *freedman,*
    ex-slave
invītāvit *invited*

5

valdē commōtus *very*
        moved, very
        much affected
paene lacrimābat *was*
        almost crying
tum *then*
excitāvit *woke up*
tōtam rem *the whole*
        story
nārrāvit *told*
parāvit *prepared*

10

Felix

Fēlīx et fūr

post cēnam Quīntus rogāvit, "pater, cūr Fēlīx nunc est lībertus? ōlim
erat servus tuus."
    tum pater tōtam rem nārrāvit.

Caecilius:	Fēlīx ōlim in tablīnō scrībēbat. Fēlīx erat sōlus.
	Clēmēns et Grumiō cibum in forō quaerēbant. 5
	Metella aberat, quod sorōrem vīsitābat.
Fēlīx:	pater tuus aberat, quod argentāriam in forō
	administrābat.
Caecilius:	nēmō erat in vīllā nisi Fēlīx et īnfāns. parvus
	īnfāns in cubiculō dormiēbat. subitō fūr per 10
	iānuam intrāvit. fūr tacitē ātrium
	circumspectāvit; tacitē cubiculum intrāvit, ubi
	īnfāns erat. Fēlīx nihil audīvit, quod intentē
	labōrābat. fūr parvum īnfantem ē vīllā tacitē
	portābat. subitō īnfāns vāgīvit. Fēlīx, postquam 15
	clāmōrem audīvit, statim ē tablīnō festīnāvit.
	"furcifer!" clāmāvit Fēlīx īrātus, et fūrem
	ferōciter pulsāvit. Fēlīx fūrem paene necāvit.
	ita Fēlīx parvum īnfantem servāvit.
Fēlīx:	dominus, postquam rem audīvit, erat laetus et 20
	mē līberāvit. ego igitur sum lībertus.
Quīntus:	sed quis erat īnfāns?
Caecilius:	erat Quīntus!

fūr *thief*

post *after*
rogāvit *asked*
nunc *now*

ōlim *once, some time ago*
sōlus *alone*
aberat *was out*
sorōrem *sister*
administrābat *was looking
after*
nisi *except*
īnfāns *child, baby*
parvus *little, small*
tacitē *quietly*
ubi *where*
nihil *nothing*
portābat *began to carry*
vāgīvit *cried, wailed*
statim *at once*
necāvit *killed*
ita *in this way*
servāvit *saved*
līberāvit *freed, set free*
igitur *therefore, and so*

About the language

1 All the stories in the first five Stages were set in the present, and in every sentence the verbs were in the **present tense**. Study the following examples:

PRESENT TENSE

singular	servus **labōrat**.	*The slave works* or *The slave is working.*
plural	servī **labōrant**.	*The slaves work* or *The slaves are working.*

2 In Stage 6, because the stories happened in the past, you have met the **imperfect tense** and the **perfect tense**. Study the different endings of the two past tenses and their English translation:

IMPERFECT TENSE

singular	poēta **recitābat**.	*A poet was reciting.*
	Metella in hortō **sedēbat**.	*Metella was sitting in the garden.*
plural	servī in forō **ambulābant**.	*The slaves were walking in the forum.*
	Pompēiānī vīnum **bibēbant**.	*The Pompeians were drinking wine.*

PERFECT TENSE

singular	ancilla **intrāvit**.	*The slave girl entered.*
	Clēmēns clāmōrem **audīvit**.	*Clemens heard the uproar.*
plural	amīcī Caecilium **salūtāvērunt**.	*The friends greeted Caecilius.*
	iuvenēs ad tabernam **festīnāvērunt**.	*The young men hurried to an inn.*

3 Compare the endings of the imperfect and perfect tenses with the endings of the present tense.

	singular	*plural*
PRESENT	portat	portant
IMPERFECT	portābat	portābant
PERFECT	portāvit	portāvērunt

You can see that in the imperfect and perfect tenses, as with the present tense, the singular ends in **-t** and the plural in **-nt**.

4 Notice how Latin shows the difference between "is," "are"
and "was," "were."

	singular	plural
PRESENT	Lūcia **est** in tablīnō.	fēminae **sunt** in culīnā.
	Lucia is in the study.	*The women are in the kitchen.*
IMPERFECT	Lūcia **erat** in forō.	fēminae **erant** in viā.
	Lucia was in the forum.	*The women were in the street.*

5 In the following examples you will see that the imperfect
tense is often used of an action or situation which was going
on for some time.

īnfāns in cubiculō **dormiēbat**. pater et māter **aberant**.
The baby was sleeping in the bedroom. *The father and mother were away.*

6 The perfect tense, on the other hand, is often used of a completed
action or an action that happened once.

agricola mercātōrem **pulsāvit**. Pompēiānī agricolam **laudāvērunt**.
The farmer punched the merchant. *The Pompeians praised the farmer.*

This well-preserved bar at Herculaneum gives us a good impression of the taberna where Clemens met Felix.

1 When you have read the following story, answer the questions opposite.

avārus

duo fūrēs ōlim ad vīllam contendēbant. in vīllā mercātor
habitābat. mercātor erat senex et avārus. avārus multam
pecūniam habēbat. fūrēs, postquam vīllam intrāvērunt,
ātrium circumspectāvērunt.

"avārus," inquit fūr, "est sōlus. avārus servum nōn habet." 5
tum fūrēs tablīnum intrāvērunt. avārus clāmāvit et
ferōciter pugnāvit, sed fūrēs senem facile superāvērunt.
"ubi est pecūnia, senex?" rogāvit fūr.
"servus fidēlis pecūniam in cubiculō custōdit," inquit senex.
"tū servum fidēlem nōn habēs, quod avārus es," clāmāvit 10
fūr. tum fūrēs cubiculum petīvērunt.
"pecūniam videō," inquit fūr. fūrēs cubiculum intrāvērunt,
ubi pecūnia erat, et pecūniam intentē spectāvērunt. sed ēheu!
ingēns serpēns in pecūniā iacēbat. fūrēs serpentem timēbant
et ē vīllā celeriter festīnāvērunt. 15
in vīllā avārus rīdēbat et serpentem laudābat.
"tū es optimus servus. numquam dormīs. pecūniam
meam semper servās."

avārus	*miser*
duo	*two*
habitābat	*was living*
inquit	*said*
pugnāvit	*fought*
facile	*easily*
fidēlis	*faithful*
custōdit	*is guarding*
ingēns	*huge*
serpēns	*snake*
iacēbat	*was lying*
timēbant	*were afraid of, feared*
celeriter	*quickly*
numquam	*never*
servās	*look after*

ingēns serpēns.

Questions

1 Who was hurrying to the merchant's house?

2 In lines 2 and 3, there is a description of the merchant. Write down three details about him.

3 What did the thieves do immediately after entering the house?

4 In line 5, why did one of the thieves think the merchant would be alone?

5 In line 7, which two Latin words tell you that the merchant resisted the thieves? Why did he lose the fight?

6 In line 9, who did the merchant say was guarding his money? Why did the thief think he was lying?

7 Which room did the thieves then enter? What did they see there?

8 Why did the thieves run away, lines 14–15?

9 In lines 17–18, how did the merchant describe the **serpēns**? What reasons did he give?

10 In line 6, the thieves found the merchant in his study. What do you think he was doing there?

2 Write out each sentence, completing it with the correct form of the noun from the parentheses. Then translate the Latin sentence. Take care with the meaning of the tenses of the verb.

For example: . . . . in forō ambulābat. (servus, servī)
servus in forō ambulābat.
The slave was walking in the forum.

. . . . forum intrāvērunt. (amīcus, amīcī)
amīcī forum intrāvērunt.
The friends entered the forum.

a . . . . per viam festīnābat. (lībertus, lībertī)
b . . . . pecūniam portābant. (ancilla, ancillae)
c . . . . ātrium circumspectāvit. (fūr, fūrēs)
d . . . . clāmōrem audīvērunt. (mercātor, mercātōrēs)
e . . . . fūrem superāvērunt. (puer, puerī)
f . . . . ad urbem festīnāvit. (nauta, nautae)

Slaves and freedmen

Wherever you traveled in the Roman world, you would find people who were slaves, like Grumio, Clemens, and Melissa. They belonged to a master or mistress, to whom they had to give complete obedience; they were not free to make decisions for themselves; they could not marry; nor could they own personal possessions or be protected by courts of law. The law, in fact, did not regard them as human beings, but as things that could be bought and sold, treated well or treated badly, according to the whim of their master. These people carried out much of the hard manual work but they also took part in many skilled trades and occupations. They did not live separately from free people; many slaves would live in the same house as their master, usually occupying rooms in the rear part of the house. Slaves and free people could often be found working together.

The Romans and others who lived around the Mediterranean in classical times regarded slavery as a normal and necessary part of life. Even those who realized that it was not a natural state of affairs made no serious attempt to abolish it.

In the Roman empire, slavery was not based on racial prejudice, and color itself did not signify slavery or obstruct advancement. People usually became slaves as a result either of being taken prisoner in war or of being captured by pirates; the children of slaves were automatically born into slavery. They came from many different tribes and countries, Gaul and Britain, Spain and North Africa, Egypt, different parts of Greece and Asia Minor, Syria and Palestine. By the time of the Emperor Augustus at the beginning of the first century AD, there were perhaps as many as three slaves for every five free citizens in Italy. Most families owned at least one or two; a merchant like Caecilius would have no fewer than a dozen in his house and many more working on his estates and in his businesses. Very wealthy men

Many people became slaves when captured in Rome's numerous wars. The scene on the left shows captives after a battle, sitting among the captured weapons and waiting to be sold. Families would be split up and slaves would be given new names by their masters.

owned hundreds and sometimes even thousands of slaves. A man called Pedanius Secundus, who lived in Rome, kept four hundred in his house there; when one of them murdered him, they were all put to death, in spite of protests by the people of Rome.

The work and treatment of slaves

Some slaves were owned privately by a **dominus** like Caecilius. Others were owned publicly, by the town council, for example. Slaves were employed in all kinds of work. In the country, their life was rougher and harsher than in the cities. They worked as laborers on farms, as shepherds and ranchers on the big estates in southern Italy, in the mines, and on the building of roads and bridges. Some of the strongest slaves were bought for training as gladiators.

In the towns, slaves were used for both unskilled and skilled work. They were cooks and gardeners, general servants, laborers in factories, secretaries, musicians, actors, and entertainers. In the course of doing such jobs, they were regularly in touch with their masters and other free men; they moved without restriction about the streets of the towns, went shopping, visited temples, and were also quite often present in the theater and at shows in the amphitheater. Foreign visitors to Rome and Italy were sometimes surprised that there was so little visible difference between a slave and a poor free man.

Some masters were cruel and brutal to their slaves, but others were kind and humane. Common sense usually prevented a master from treating his slaves too harshly, since only fit, well-cared-for slaves were likely to work efficiently. A slave who was a skilled craftsman, particularly one who was able to read and write, keep accounts, and manage the work of a small shop, would have cost a large sum of money; and a sensible master would not waste an expensive possession through carelessness.

Slaves' jobs varied from serving drinks in the home and nursing children, to heavy labor, such as transporting goods.

Some were trained as gladiators.

Masters were free to beat unsatisfactory slaves. House slaves were often punished by being sent to work on the owner's farm.

Freeing a slave

Not all slaves remained in slavery until they died. Freedom was sometimes given as a reward for particularly good service, sometimes as a sign of friendship and respect. A slave might also buy his freedom. (Although the law said that slaves could not own personal possessions, a slave might amass assets such as money, goods, and land.)

Freedom was also very commonly given after the owner's death by a statement in the will. But the law laid down certain limits. For example, a slave could not be freed before he was thirty years old; and not more than a hundred slaves (fewer in a small household) could be freed in a will.

The act of freeing a slave was called **manūmissiō**. This word is connected with two other words, **manus** (hand) and **mittō** (send), and means "a sending out from the hand" or "setting free from control." Manumission was performed in several ways. The oldest method took the form of a legal ceremony before a public official, such as a judge. This is the ceremony seen in the picture at the beginning of this Stage. A witness claimed that the slave did not really belong to the master at all; the master did not deny the claim; the slave's head was then touched with a rod and he was declared officially free. There were other, simpler methods. A master might manumit a slave by making a declaration in the presence of friends at home or merely by an invitation to recline on the couch at dinner.

Freedmen and freedwomen

The ex-slave became a **lībertus** (freedman). He now had the opportunity to make his own way in life, and possibly to become an important member of his community. He did not, however, receive all the privileges of a citizen who had been born free. He could not stand as a candidate in public elections, nor could he become a high-ranking officer in the army. He still had obligations to his former master and had to work for him a fixed number of days each year. He would become one of his clients and would visit him regularly to pay his respects, usually early in the morning. He would be expected to help and support his former master whenever he could. This connection between them is seen very clearly in the names taken by a freedman. Suppose that his slave name had been Felix and his master had been Lucius Caecilius Iucundus. As soon as he was freed, Felix would take some of the names of his former master and call himself Lucius Caecilius Felix.

Some freedmen continued to do the same work that they had previously done as slaves; others were set up in business by their former masters. Others became priests in the temples or servants of the town council; the council secretaries, messengers, town clerk, and town crier were all probably freedmen. Some became very rich and powerful. Two freedmen at Pompeii, who were called the Vettii and were possibly brothers, owned a house which is one of the most magnificent in the town. The colorful paintings on its walls and the elegant marble fountains in the garden show clearly how prosperous the Vettii were. Another Pompeian freedman was the architect who designed the large theater; another was the father of Lucius Caecilius Iucundus.

A female ex-slave was called a **līberta**. Like freedmen, many freedwomen earned their living using the skills they had learnt as slaves. Some stayed in the house where they had been slaves and may have worked as hairdressers, seamstresses, or nurses. Some freedwomen married their former masters. Others are known to have worked as shopkeepers, artisans, and even moneylenders.

The peristylium of the House of the Vettii.

Vocabulary checklist 6

abest	*is out, is absent*
aberat	*was out, was absent*
cubiculum	*bedroom*
emit	*buys*
ferōciter	*fiercely*
festīnat	*hurries*
fortis	*brave*
fūr	*thief*
intentē	*intently, carefully*
lībertus	*freedman, ex-slave*
ōlim	*once, some time ago*
parvus	*small*
per	*through*
postquam	*after*
pulsat	*hits, punches*
quod	*because*
rēs	*thing*
scrībit	*writes*
subitō	*suddenly*
superat	*overcomes, overpowers*
tum	*then*
tuus	*your, yours*
vēndit	*sells*
vituperat	*blames, curses*

The two freedmen called the Vettii had their best dining room decorated with tiny pictures of cupids, seen here racing in chariots drawn by deer.

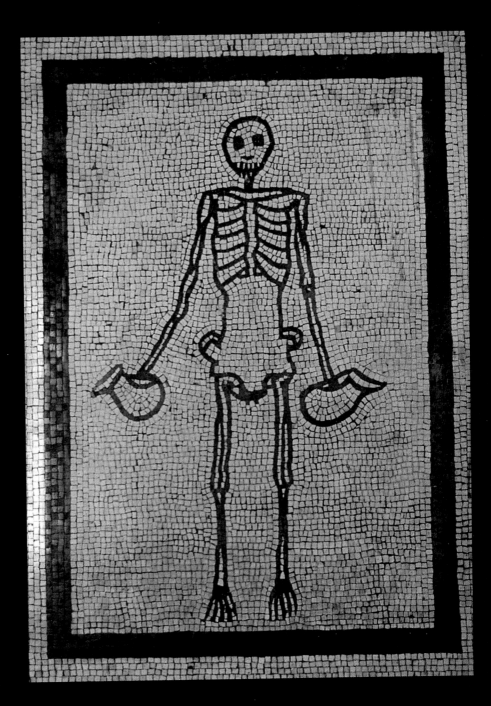

CENA

Stage 7

cēna

1   amīcus Caecilium vīsitābat.
    vīllam intrāvit.

2   Caecilius amīcum exspectābat.
    amīcum salūtāvit.

3   amīcus cum Caeciliō cēnābat.
    cēnam laudāvit.

4   poēta triclīnium intrāvit.
    versum recitāvit.

5 amīcus pōculum īnspexit.
   vīnum gustāvit.

6 amīcus pōculum hausit.
   tum fābulam longam nārrāvit.

7 Caecilius plausit.
   "euge!" dīxit.

8 amīcī optimum vīnum bibērunt.
   tandem surrēxērunt.

9 servī in ātriō stābant.
   iānuam aperuērunt.

10 amīcus "valē" dīxit.
   ē vīllā discessit.

fābula mīrābilis

multī amīcī cum Caeciliō et cum Metellā cēnābant. Fēlīx quoque
aderat. omnēs amīcī coquum laudāvērunt, quod cēna erat optima.

postquam omnēs cēnāvērunt, Caecilius clāmāvit, "ubi est
Decēns? Decēns nōn adest." tum Caecilius Clēmentem ē vīllā
mīsit. servus Decentem per urbem quaesīvit.

postquam servus ē vīllā discessit, Fēlīx pōculum hausit. tum
lībertus fābulam mīrābilem nārrāvit:

"ōlim amīcus meus ex urbe discēdēbat. nox erat, sed lūna
plēna lūcēbat. amīcus per viam festīnābat, ubi silva erat, et
subitō centuriōnem cōnspexit. amīcus meus centuriōnem
salūtāvit. centuriō tamen nihil dīxit. tum centuriō tunicam
dēposuit. ecce! centuriō ēvānuit. ingēns lupus subitō appāruit.
amīcus meus valdē timēbat. ingēns lupus ululāvit et ad silvam
festīnāvit. tunica in viā iacēbat. amīcus tunicam cautē īnspexit.
ecce! tunica erat lapidea. tum amīcus rem intellēxit. centuriō
erat versipellis."

5

10

15

fābula	*story*
mīrābilis	*strange*
mīsit	*sent*
discessit	*departed, left*
pōculum hausit	*drained his wine cup*
ex urbe	*from the city*
nox erat	*it was night*
lūna plēna	*full moon*
lūcēbat	*was shining*
silva	*woods, forest*
centuriōnem	*centurion*
cōnspexit	*caught sight of*
dīxit	*said*
tunicam	*tunic*
dēposuit	*took off*
ēvānuit	*vanished*
lupus	*wolf*
appāruit	*appeared*
ululāvit	*howled*
cautē	*cautiously*
īnspexit	*looked at, examined*
lapidea	*made of stone*
rem intellēxit	*understood the truth*
versipellis	*werewolf*

About the language 1

1 Study the following example:

> mercātor Caecilium vīsitābat. mercātor vīllam intrāvit.
> *A merchant was visiting Caecilius. The merchant entered the house.*

2 In Stage 7, you have met a shorter way of saying this:

> mercātor Caecilium vīsitābat. vīllam intrāvit.
> *A merchant was visiting Caecilius.* **He** *entered the house.*

The following sentences behave in the same way:

> amīcī cum Caeciliō cēnābant. coquum laudāvērunt.
> *Friends were dining with Caecilius.* **They** *praised the cook.*

> ancilla in ātriō stābat. dominum salūtāvit.
> *The slave girl was standing in the atrium.* **She** *greeted the master.*

3 Notice that Latin does not have to include a separate word for "he," "she," or "they." **intrāvit** can mean "he entered" or "she entered," depending on the context.

4 Further examples:

  a Grumiō in culīnā labōrābat. cēnam parābat.
  b āctōrēs in theātrō clāmābant. fābulam agēbant.
  c Metella nōn erat in vīllā. in hortō ambulābat.
  d lībertī in tabernā bibēbant. Grumiōnem salūtāvērunt.
  e iuvenis pōculum hausit. vīnum laudāvit.
  f puellae in viā stābant. lupum audīvērunt.

Part of a mosaic floor, showing the scraps left behind by the diners after a cena.

Decēns

postquam Fēlīx fābulam nārrāvit, omnēs plausērunt. tum hospitēs tacēbant et aliam fābulam exspectābant. subitō clāmōrem audīvērunt. omnēs ad ātrium festīnāvērunt, ubi Clēmēns stābat.

Caecilius:	hercle! quid est? cūr tū clāmōrem facis?	
Clēmēns:	Decēns, Decēns …	5
Caecilius:	quid est?	
Clēmēns:	Decēns est mortuus.	
omnēs:	quid? mortuus? ēheu!	
	(duo servī intrant.)	
Caecilius:	quid dīcis?	10
servus prīmus:	dominus meus ad vīllam tuam veniēbat; dominus gladiātōrem prope amphitheātrum cōnspexit.	
servus secundus:	gladiātor dominum terruit, quod gladium ingentem vibrābat. tum gladiātor clāmāvit, "tū mē nōn terrēs, leō, tū mē nōn terrēs! leōnēs amīcum meum in arēnā necāvērunt, sed tū mē nōn terrēs!"	15
servus prīmus:	Decēns valdē timēbat. "tū es īnsānus," inquit dominus. "ego nōn sum leō. sum homō."	20
servus secundus:	gladiātor tamen dominum ferōciter petīvit et eum ad amphitheātrum trāxit. dominus perterritus clāmāvit. Clēmēns clāmōrem audīvit.	
servus prīmus:	Clēmēns, quod fortis erat, amphitheātrum intrāvit. Decentem in arēnā cōnspexit. dominus meus erat mortuus.	25
Metella:	ego rem intellegō! gladiātor erat Pugnāx. Pugnāx erat gladiātor nōtissimus. Pugnāx ōlim in arēnā pugnābat, et leō Pugnācem necāvit. Pugnāx nōn vīvit; Pugnāx est umbra. umbra Decentem necāvit.	30

plausērunt	*applauded*
hospitēs	*guests*
tacēbant	*were silent*
aliam	*another*
hercle!	*by Hercules!*
	good heavens!
mortuus	*dead*
prīmus	*first*
gladiātōrem	*gladiator*
prope amphitheātrum	*near the amphitheater*
secundus	*second*
terruit	*frightened*
gladium	*sword*
vibrābat	*was brandishing, was waving*
in arēnā	*in the arena*
īnsānus	*insane, crazy*
homō	*man*
eum	*him*
trāxit	*dragged*
nōtissimus	*very well-known*
vīvit	*is alive*
umbra	*ghost*

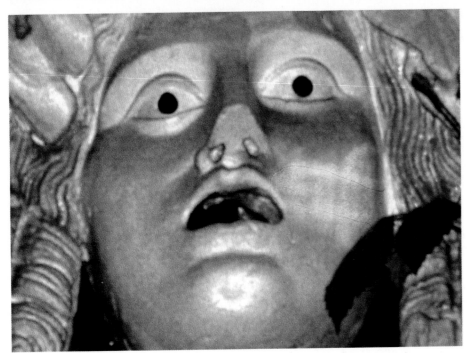

Decēns valdē timēbat.

post cēnam

postquam Metella rem explicāvit, omnēs amīcī tacēbant. mox
"valē" dīxērunt et ē vīllā discessērunt. per viam timidē
prōcēdēbant. nūllae stēllae lūcēbant. nūlla lūna erat in caelō.
amīcī nihil audīvērunt, quod viae dēsertae erant. amīcī per
urbem tacitē prōcēdēbant, quod umbram timēbant.   5

explicāvit *explained*
valē *good-bye*
timidē *nervously*
prōcēdēbant *were proceeding, were advancing*
nūllae stēllae *no stars*
in caelō *in the sky*
dēsertae *deserted*

   subitō fēlēs ululāvit. amīcī valdē timēbant. omnēs per urbem
perterritī ruērunt, quod dē vītā dēspērābant. clāmōrem
mīrābilem fēcērunt. multī Pompēiānī erant sollicitī, quod
clāmōrem audīvērunt. Caecilius et Metella clāmōrem nōn
audīvērunt, quod in cubiculō dormiēbant.   10

fēlēs *cat*
ruērunt *rushed*
dē vītā dēspērābant *were scared for their lives*
fēcērunt *made*
sollicitī *worried, anxious*

About the language 2

1 In Stage 6, you met examples of the perfect tense. They looked like this:

> senex ad tabernam **ambulāvit**.   amīcī in urbe **dormīvērunt**.
> *The old man walked to the inn.*   *The friends slept in the city.*

This is a very common way of forming the perfect tense in Latin.

2 In Stage 7, you have met other forms of the perfect tense. Look at the following examples:

PRESENT	PERFECT	
	singular	*plural*
appāret	appāruit	appāruērunt
	s/he appeared	*they appeared*
dīcit	dīxit	dīxērunt
	s/he said	*they said*
discēdit	discessit	discessērunt
	s/he left	*they left*
facit	fēcit	fēcērunt
	s/he made	*they made*

3 If you are not sure whether a particular verb is in the present tense or the perfect tense, you can check by looking it up in the Vocabulary part of the Language information section.

Symbolic of man's fate, this mosaic tabletop comes from a summer triclinium.

Metella et Melissa

Metella Melissam in vīllā quaerēbat. Metella culīnam intrāvit,
ubi Grumiō labōrābat. Grumiō erat īrātus.

"cūr tū es īrātus, Grumiō? cūr ferōciter circumspectās?"
rogāvit Metella.

"heri Melissa cēnam optimam parāvit," respondit coquus.   5
"hodiē ego cēnam pessimam parō, quod nūllus cibus adest. heri
multus cibus erat in culīnā. ancilla omnem cibum coxit."

Metella ē culīnā discessit et ad tablīnum festīnāvit, ubi
Clēmēns labōrābat. Clēmēns quoque erat īrātus.

"Melissa est pestis!" clāmāvit servus.   10

"quid fēcit Melissa?" rogāvit Metella.

"heri Melissa in tablīnō labōrābat," respondit Clēmēns. "hodiē
ego in tablīnō labōrō. ecce! cērae et stilī absunt. nihil est in locō
propriō."

Metella, postquam ē tablīnō discessit, hortum intrāvit.   15
Metella Melissam in hortō vīdit. ēheu! ancilla lacrimābat.

"Melissa, cūr lacrimās?" rogāvit Metella.

"lacrimō quod Grumiō et Clēmēns mē vituperant," respondit
ancilla.

"ego tamen tē nōn vituperō," inquit Metella. "ego tē laudō.   20
ecce! tū crīnēs meōs optimē compōnis. stolam meam optimē
compōnis. fortasse Grumiō et Clēmēns tē nōn laudant; sed ego
tē laudō, quod mē dīligenter cūrās."

heri	*yesterday*
pessimam	*very bad*
coxit	*cooked*
fēcit	*has done*
stilī	*pens (used for writing on wax tablets)*
in locō propriō	*in the right place*
vīdit	*saw*
tē	*you*
crīnēs	*hair*
optimē	*very well*
compōnis	*arrange*
stolam	*(long) dress*
fortasse	*perhaps*
dīligenter	*carefully*
cūrās	*take care of*

1 When you have read the following story, answer the questions opposite.

animal ferōx

Caecilius et Fēlīx in tablīnō sedēbant. Caecilius Fēlīcem ad vēnātiōnem invītāvit.

"ingēns aper," inquit Caecilius, "in monte Vesuviō latet. amīcī meī aprum vīdērunt. animal tamen est ferōx. amīcī eum numquam cēpērunt." 5

"ego vēnātor optimus sum," respondit Fēlīx. "aper mē nōn terret! sed cūr tū Quīntum ad vēnātiōnem nōn invītās?"

Caecilius igitur filium vocāvit. Quīntus laetissimus vēnābulum cēpit et cum patre et lībertō ad vēnātiōnem contendit. multī servī et multī canēs aderant. omnēs ad montem prōcessērunt, 10 ubi aper latēbat.

servī, postquam aprum cōnspexērunt, clāmōrem fēcērunt. aper ferōx, quod clāmōrem audīvit, impetum fēcit. Fēlīx vēnābulum ēmīsit, sed aprum nōn percussit. lībertus, quod ad terram dēcidit, clāmāvit, "ēheu! aper mē petit!" 15

Quīntus fortiter prōcessit et vēnābulum ēmīsit. ecce! aprum percussit. ingēns aper ad terram mortuus dēcidit.

"euge!" clāmāvit Caecilius. "ōlim Fēlīx Quīntum servāvit. nunc filius meus Fēlīcem servāvit!"

animal *animal*
ferōx *fierce, ferocious*

vēnātiōnem *hunt*
aper *boar*
in monte Vesuviō *on Mount Vesuvius*
latet *lies hidden*
cēpērunt *(have) caught*
vēnātor *hunter*
vēnābulum *hunting spear*
cēpit *took*
prōcessērunt *proceeded*
impetum *attack, charge*
ēmīsit *threw*
percussit *hit*
terram *ground*
dēcidit *fell down*
fortiter *bravely*

Questions

1 Whom did Caecilius invite to the hunt (lines 1–2)?
2 In lines 3 and 4, there is a description of the boar. Write down three details about it.
3 What did Caecilius say his friends had never been able to achieve?
4 In line 6, why is Felix confident that he can do what Caecilius' friends could not?
5 What additional suggestion does Felix make to Caecilius (line 7)?
6 In lines 8–9, how did Quintus equip himself for the hunt?
7 In line 13, which two Latin words tell you that the noise made by the slaves was effective?
8 Why did Felix call out for help (lines 13–15)?
9 How did Quintus respond? What did he manage to achieve?
10 In lines 18–19, Caecilius sums up the situation. What do you think he is feeling toward Quintus?

Marble statue of a stag being taken down by a group of hounds.

2 Complete each sentence with the correct phrase. Then translate
   the sentence.

   For example: amīcī . . . . (vīllam intrāvit, cēnam laudāvērunt)
               amīcī **cēnam laudāvērunt**.
               The friends praised the dinner.

   a mercātor . . . . (ē vīllā discessit, clāmōrem audīvērunt)
   b ancillae . . . . (ad vīllam ambulāvit, in vīllā dormīvērunt)
   c leōnēs . . . . (gladiātōrem terruit, gladiātōrem cōnspexērunt)
   d lībertī . . . . (lūnam spectāvit, ad portum festīnāvērunt)
   e centuriō . . . . (fābulam audīvit, servum laudāvērunt)
   f fūr . . . . (per urbem ruit, centuriōnem terruērunt)
   g Caecilius et amīcus . . . . (leōnem cōnspexit, portum petīvērunt)
   h amīcī . . . . (pōculum īnspexit, rem intellēxērunt)

3 Complete each sentence with the correct form of the noun. Then translate
   the sentence.

   For example: coquus . . . . parāvit. (cēna, cēnam)
               coquus **cēnam** parāvit.
               The cook prepared the dinner.

               . . . . ad silvam ambulāvērunt. (servus, servī)
               servī ad silvam ambulāvērunt.
               The slaves walked to the wood.

   a Clēmēns . . . . excitāvit. (dominus, dominum)
   b . . . . fābulam nārrāvit. (lībertus, lībertum)
   c . . . . gladiātōrem cōnspexērunt. (amīcus, amīcī)
   d . . . . ad forum festīnāvērunt. (agricola, agricolae)
   e ancilla . . . . aperuit. (iānua, iānuam)
   f . . . . clāmōrem fēcit. (puella, puellae)
   g fūrēs . . . . necāvērunt. (centuriō, centuriōnem)
   h . . . . cēnam laudāvit. (gladiātor, gladiātōrem)
   i . . . . cibum ad theātrum portāvērunt. (spectātor, spectātōrēs)
   j . . . . ē vīllā discessit. (senex, senēs)

Tombs outside the Herculaneum Gate.

Roman beliefs about life after death

The Romans usually placed the tombs of the dead by the side of roads just outside towns. The tombs at Pompeii can still be seen along the roads that go north from the Herculaneum Gate and south from the Nuceria Gate.

Some tombs were grand and impressive and looked like small houses; others were plain and simple. Inside a tomb there was a chest or vase containing the ashes of the dead person; sometimes there were recesses in the walls of a tomb to hold the remains of several members of a family. The ashes of poor people, who could not afford the expense of a tomb, were buried more simply. At this time cremation was the normal way of disposing of the dead.

In building their cemeteries along busy roads, and not in peaceful and secluded places, the Romans were not showing any lack of respect. On the contrary, they believed that unless the dead were properly treated, their ghosts would haunt the living and possibly do them harm. It was most important to provide the dead with a tomb or grave, where their ghosts could have a home. But it was also thought that they would want to be close to the life of the living. One tomb has this inscription: "I see and gaze upon all who come to and from the city" and another, "Lollius has been placed by the side of the road in order that everyone who passes may say to him 'Hello, Lollius.'"

Inside a Pompeian tomb, with recesses for the ashes.

It was believed that the dead in some way continued the activities of life, and therefore had to be supplied with the things they would need. A craftsman would want his tools, a woman her jewelry, children their toys. When the bodies of the dead were cremated, their possessions were burned or buried with them.

A Greek writer called Lucian tells the story of a husband who had burned all his dead wife's jewelry and clothes on the funeral pyre, so that she might have them in the next world. A week later he was trying to comfort himself by reading a book about life after death, when the ghost of his wife appeared. She began to reproach him because he had not burned one of her gilt sandals, which, she said, was lying under a chest. The family dog then barked and the ghost disappeared. The husband looked under the chest, found the sandal, and burned it. The ghost was now content and did not appear again.

The ghosts of the dead were also thought to be hungry and thirsty, and therefore had to be given food and drink. Offerings of eggs, beans, lentils, flour, and wine were placed regularly at the tomb. Sometimes holes were made in the tomb so that food and wine could be poured inside. Wine was a convenient substitute for blood, the favorite drink of the dead. At the funeral and on special occasions animals were sacrificed, and their blood was offered.

Section through a Roman burial in Caerleon, Wales. A pipe ran down into the container for the ashes so that gifts of food and drink could be poured in.

Cremation urns

Ashes were buried in containers of many materials, including stone, metal, and glass. One wealthy Pompeian had his ashes buried in this fabulously expensive, hand-carved blue and white glass vase, which was found in one of the tombs outside the Herculaneum Gate. Poor people might put the ashes of the dead in secondhand storage jars which were then buried in the earth.

It was thought, however, that in spite of these attempts to look after them, the dead did not lead a very happy existence. In order to help them forget their unhappiness, their tombs were often decorated with flowers and surrounded by little gardens, a custom which has lasted to this day, although its original meaning has changed. With the same purpose in mind, the family and friends of a dead person held a banquet after the funeral and on the anniversary of the death. Sometimes these banquets took place in a dining room attached to the tomb itself, sometimes in the family home. The ghosts of the dead were thought to attend and enjoy these cheerful occasions.

An open-air dining room attached to a tomb outside the Herculaneum Gate, where the relatives could feast with the dead.

In addition to these ceremonies two festivals for the dead were held every year. At one of these, families remembered parents and relations who had died; at the other, they performed rites to exorcise any ghosts in their houses who might be lonely or hungry and therefore dangerous.

Some people also believed in the Greek myths about the underworld where the wicked were punished for their crimes and where the good lived happily forever.

There were a few people who did not believe in any form of life after death. These were the followers of a Greek philosopher called Epicurus, who taught that when a man died the breath that gave him life dissolved in the air and was lost forever.

Most Romans, however, felt no need to question their traditional beliefs and customs, which kept the dead alive in their memories and ensured that their spirits were happy and at peace.

A bronze head of Epicurus, from a villa at Herculaneum.

Vocabulary checklist 7

cēnat: cēnāvit	*eats dinner, dines*
cōnspicit: cōnspexit	*catches sight of*
cum	*with*
facit: fēcit	*makes, does*
heri	*yesterday*
ingēns	*huge*
intellegit: intellēxit	*understands*
lacrimat: lacrimāvit	*weeps, cries*
mortuus	*dead*
nārrat: nārrāvit	*tells, relates*
necat: necāvit	*kills*
nihil	*nothing*
omnis	*all*
parat: parāvit	*prepares*
prope	*near*
rogat: rogāvit	*asks*
tacitē	*quietly*
tamen	*however*
terret: terruit	*frightens*
valdē	*very much, very*

Dead sinners being punished in the underworld: Sisyphus had to roll a stone forever, Ixion was tied to a revolving wheel, and Tantalus was never able to quench his raging thirst.

GLADIATORES

Stage 8

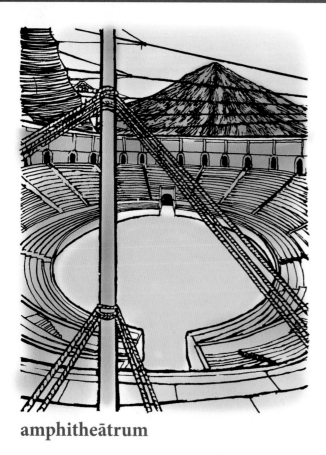

amphitheātrum

1 nūntiī spectāculum nūntiābant.
  Pompēiānī nūntiōs audiēbant.

2 gladiātōrēs per viam prōcēdēbant.
  Pompēiānī gladiātōrēs laudābant.

3 puellae iuvenēs salūtāvērunt. iuvenēs
  quoque ad amphitheātrum contendēbant.

4 servī fēminās spectābant, quod fēminae ad spectāculum contendēbant.

5 puerī per viam festīnābant. puellae puerōs salūtāvērunt.

6 Pompēiānī tabernās nōn intrāvērunt, quod tabernae erant clausae.

7 postquam gladiātōrēs Pompēiānōs salūtāvērunt, Pompēiānī plausērunt.

8 Pompēiānī gladiātōrēs intentē spectābant, quod gladiātōrēs in arēnā pugnābant.

9 spectātōrēs murmillōnēs incitābant, quod murmillōnēs saepe victōrēs erant.

gladiātōrēs

Rēgulus erat senātor Rōmānus. in vīllā magnificā habitābat. vīlla
erat prope Nūceriam. Nūcerīnī et Pompēiānī erant inimīcī.
Nūcerīnī, quod amphitheātrum nōn habēbant, saepe ad
amphitheātrum Pompēiānum veniēbant; saepe erant turbulentī.

Rēgulus ōlim spectāculum splendidum in amphitheātrō   5
ēdidit, quod diem nātālem celebrābat. multī Nūcerīnī igitur ad
urbem vēnērunt. cīvēs Pompēiānī erant īrātī, quod Nūcerīnī viās
complēbant. omnēs tamen ad forum contendērunt, ubi nūntiī
stābant. nūntiī spectāculum optimum nūntiābant:

"gladiātōrēs adsunt! vīgintī gladiātōrēs hodiē pugnant!   10
rētiāriī adsunt! murmillōnēs adsunt! bēstiāriī bēstiās ferōcēs
agitant!"

Pompēiānī, postquam nūntiōs audīvērunt, ad amphitheātrum
quam celerrimē contendērunt. Nūcerīnī quoque ad
amphitheātrum festīnāvērunt. omnēs vehementer clāmābant.   15
Pompēiānī et Nūcerīnī, postquam amphitheātrum intrāvērunt,
tacuērunt. prīmam pugnam exspectābant.

senātor Rōmānus
  a Roman senator
magnificā *magnificent*
Nūceriam *Nuceria (a town
  near Pompeii)*
Nūcerīnī *the people of
  Nuceria*
inimīcī *enemies*
saepe *often*
turbulentī *rowdy, disorderly*
spectāculum *show, spectacle*
splendidum *splendid*
ēdidit *presented*
diem nātālem *birthday*
celebrābat *was celebrating*
vēnērunt *came*
cīvēs *citizens*
complēbant *were filling*
nūntiābant *were announcing*
vīgintī *twenty*
rētiāriī *net fighters*
murmillōnēs *heavily armed
  gladiators*
bēstiāriī *beast fighters*
bēstiās *beasts*
quam celerrimē *as quickly
  as possible*
vehementer *loudly, violently*
tacuērunt *fell silent*

*The amphitheater at Pompeii. Notice one
of the staircases that led up to the top seats.
The public sports ground is behind the trees
on the right. On performance days, the open
space would have been full of stalls selling
refreshments and souvenirs.*

A retiarius with his trident, net, and protection for his right arm and neck.

in arēnā

duo rētiāriī et duo murmillōnēs arēnam intrāvērunt. postquam
gladiātōrēs spectātōrēs salūtāvērunt, tuba sonuit. tum
gladiātōrēs pugnam commīsērunt. murmillōnēs Pompēiānōs
valdē dēlectābant, quod saepe victōrēs erant. Pompēiānī igitur
murmillōnēs incitābant. sed rētiāriī, quod erant expedītī,
murmillōnēs facile ēvītāvērunt.

    "rētiāriī nōn pugnant! rētiāriī sunt ignāvī!" clāmāvērunt
Pompēiānī. Nūcerīnī tamen respondērunt, "rētiāriī sunt callidī!
rētiāriī murmillōnēs dēcipiunt!"

    murmillōnēs rētiāriōs frūstrā ad pugnam prōvocāvērunt. tum
murmillō clāmāvit, "ūnus murmillō facile duōs rētiāriōs superat."

    Pompēiānī plausērunt. tum murmillō rētiāriōs statim petīvit.
murmillō et rētiāriī ferōciter pugnāvērunt. rētiāriī tandem
murmillōnem graviter vulnerāvērunt. tum rētiāriī alterum
murmillōnem petīvērunt. hic murmillō fortiter pugnāvit, sed
rētiāriī eum quoque superāvērunt.

    Pompēiānī, quod īrātī erant, murmillōnēs vituperābant;
missiōnem tamen postulābant, quod murmillōnēs fortēs erant.
Nūcerīnī mortem postulābant. omnēs spectātōrēs tacēbant, et
Rēgulum intentē spectābant. Rēgulus, quod Nūcerīnī mortem
postulābant, pollicem vertit. Pompēiānī erant īrātī, et
vehementer clāmābant. rētiāriī tamen, postquam Rēgulus
signum dedit, murmillōnēs interfēcērunt.

5

10

15

20

tuba *trumpet*
sonuit *sounded*
pugnam commīsērunt
        began the fight
victōrēs *victors, winners*
expedītī *lightly armed*
ēvītāvērunt *avoided*
ignāvī *cowardly*
callidī *clever*
dēcipiunt *are deceiving,*
        are tricking
frūstrā *in vain*
prōvocāvērunt *challenged*
ūnus *one*
graviter *seriously*
vulnerāvērunt *wounded*
alterum *the second, the*
        other
hic *this*
missiōnem *release*
mortem *death*
pollicem vertit *turned*
        his thumb up
dedit *gave*
interfēcērunt *killed*

1 From Stage 2 onwards, you have met sentences like these:

> amīcus **puellam** salūtat.   The friend greets the girl.
> dominus **servum** vituperābat.   The master was cursing the slave.
> nautae **mercātōrem** laudāvērunt.   The sailors praised the merchant.

In each of these examples, the person who has something done to him or her is indicated in Latin by the **accusative singular**.

2 In Stage 8, you have met sentences like these:

> amīcus **puellās** salūtat.   The friend greets the girls.
> dominus **servōs** vituperābat.   The master was cursing the slaves.
> nautae **mercātōrēs** laudāvērunt.   The sailors praised the merchants.

In these examples, the persons who have something done to them are indicated in Latin by the **accusative plural**.

3 You have now met the following cases:

SINGULAR			
nominative	puella	servus	mercātor
accusative	puellam	servum	mercātōrem

PLURAL			
nominative	puellae	servī	mercātōrēs
accusative	puellās	servōs	mercātōrēs

4 Further examples:

  a ancilla gladiātōrem laudāvit. ancilla gladiātōrēs laudāvit.
  b servus ancillam interfēcit. servus ancillās interfēcit.
  c centuriō servōs laudāvit.
  d puer āctōrēs ad theātrum dūxit.
  e senex āctōrem ad forum dūxit.
  f amīcus fābulās nārrāvit.
  g fēminae cibum gustāvērunt.
  h agricolae nūntiōs audīvērunt.

vēnātiō

When you have read this story, answer the questions at the end.

postquam rētiāriī ex arēnā discessērunt, tuba iterum sonuit. subitō multī cervī arēnam intrāvērunt. cervī per tōtam arēnam currēbant, quod perterritī erant. tum canēs ferōcēs per portam intrāvērunt. canēs statim cervōs perterritōs agitāvērunt et interfēcērunt. postquam canēs cervōs superāvērunt, lupī arēnam intrāvērunt. lupī, quod valdē ēsuriēbant, canēs ferōciter petīvērunt. canēs erant fortissimī, sed lupī facile canēs superāvērunt.

    Nūcerīnī erant laetissimī et Rēgulum laudābant. Pompēiānī tamen nōn erant contentī, sed clāmābant, "ubi sunt leōnēs? cūr Rēgulus leōnēs retinet?"

    Rēgulus, postquam hunc clāmōrem audīvit, signum dedit. statim trēs leōnēs per portam ruērunt. tuba iterum sonuit. bēstiāriī arēnam audācissimē intrāvērunt. leōnēs tamen bēstiāriōs nōn petīvērunt. leōnēs in arēnā recubuērunt. leōnēs obdormīvērunt!

    tum Pompēiānī erant īrātissimī, quod Rēgulus spectāculum rīdiculum ēdēbat. Pompēiānī Rēgulum et Nūcerīnōs ex amphitheātrō agitāvērunt. Nūcerīnī per viās fugiēbant, quod valdē timēbant. Pompēiānī tamen gladiōs suōs dēstrīnxērunt et multōs Nūcerīnōs interfēcērunt. ecce! sanguis nōn in arēnā sed per viās fluēbat.

	iterum *again*
	cervī *deer*
5	**ēsuriēbant** *were hungry*
	fortissimī *very brave*
	retinet *is holding back*
	hunc *this*
	trēs *three*
10	**audācissimē** *very boldly*
	recubuērunt *lay down*
	obdormīvērunt *went to sleep*
	īrātissimī *very angry*
15	**rīdiculum** *ridiculous, silly*
	ēdēbat *was presenting*
	fugiēbant *began to run away, began to flee*
20	**suōs** *their*
	dēstrīnxērunt *drew*

Questions

1 **postquam … intrāvērunt** (lines 1–2). What happened after the retiarii left the arena?
2 In lines 4–5, how did the deer feel and what happened to them?
3 In lines 6–8, why did the wolves chase the dogs? How did the chase end?
4 In lines 9–10, what were the different feelings of the Nucerians and Pompeians?
5 Why were the Pompeians feeling like this?
6 **Rēgulus … signum dedit** (line 12). What happened next?
7 When the beast fighters entered the arena in lines 13–14, what would you have expected to happen? What went wrong?
8 Why were the Pompeians angry and what did they do?
9 **Pompēiānī … interfēcērunt** (lines 19–20). What made the riot so serious?
10 Read the last sentence. Why do you think **ecce!** is put in front of it?

pāstor et leō

ōlim pāstor in silvā ambulābat. subitō pāstor leōnem cōnspexit.
leō tamen pāstōrem nōn agitāvit. leō lacrimābat! pāstor,
postquam leōnem cōnspexit, erat attonitus et rogāvit,

    "cūr lacrimās, leō? cūr mē nōn agitās? cūr mē nōn cōnsūmis?"

    leō trīstis pedem ostendit. pāstor spīnam in pede cōnspexit,   5
tum clāmāvit,

    "ego spīnam videō! spīnam ingentem videō! nunc intellegō!
tū lacrimās, quod pēs dolet."

    pāstor, quod benignus et fortis erat, ad leōnem cautē vēnit et
spīnam īnspexit. leō fremuit, quod ignāvus erat.   10

    "leō!" exclāmāvit pāstor, "ego perterritus sum, quod tū fremis.
sed tē adiuvō. ecce! spīna!"

    postquam hoc dīxit, pāstor spīnam quam celerrimē extrāxit.
leō ignāvus iterum fremuit et ē silvā festīnāvit.

    posteā, Rōmānī hunc pāstōrem comprehendērunt, quod   15
Christiānus erat, et eum ad arēnam dūxērunt. postquam arēnam
intrāvit, pāstor spectātōrēs vīdit et valdē timēbat. tum pāstor
bēstiās vīdit et clāmāvit, "nunc mortuus sum! videō leōnēs et
lupōs. ēheu!"

    tum ingēns leō ad eum ruit. leō, postquam pāstōrem olfēcit,   20
nōn eum cōnsūmpsit sed lambēbat! pāstor attonitus leōnem
agnōvit et dīxit,

    "tē agnōscō! tū es leō trīstis! spīna erat in pede tuō."

    leō iterum fremuit, et pāstōrem ex arēnā ad salūtem dūxit.

attonitus *astonished*

trīstis *sad*
pedem *foot, paw*
ostendit *showed*
spīnam *thorn*
dolet *hurts*
benignus *kind*
fremuit *roared*
exclāmāvit *shouted*
adiuvō *help*
hoc *this*
extrāxit *pulled out*
posteā *afterwards*
comprehendērunt
             arrested
Christiānus *Christian*
olfēcit *smelled, sniffed*
lambēbat *began to lick*
agnōvit *recognized*

ad salūtem *to safety*

About the language 2

1 Study the following pairs of sentences:

Pompēiānī erant īrātī.   Pompēiānī erant **īrātissimī**.
The Pompeians were angry.   *The Pompeians were very angry.*

gladiātor est nōtus.   gladiātor est **nōtissimus**.
The gladiator is famous.   *The gladiator is very famous.*

māter erat laeta.   māter erat **laetissima**.
The mother was happy.   *The mother was very happy.*

The words in **boldface** are known as superlatives. Notice how they are translated in the examples above.

2 Further examples:

a mercātor est trīstis. senex est trīstissimus.
b canis erat ferōx. leō erat ferōcissimus.
c fīlia fābulam longissimam nārrāvit.
d murmillōnēs erant fortēs, sed rētiāriī erant fortissimī.

Gladiator fights were show business, and were performed to the sound of trumpet and organ.

A duel reaches its climax in this painting from a tomb at Pompeii.

1 Complete each sentence with the correct word from the box.
  Then translate the sentence.

  a . . . . multās vīllās habeō.
  b ego servōs . . . .
  c tū gladiātōrēs . . . .
  d ego . . . . salūtō.
  e . . . . ancillās laudās.
  f tū . . . . agitās.

ego	leōnēs
tū	vēndō
amīcōs	spectās

2 Complete each sentence with the correct form of the verb from the parentheses.
  Then translate the sentence.

  a tū es vēnālīcius; tū servōs in forō . . . . (vēndō, vēndis, vēndit)
  b ego sum gladiātor; ego in arēnā . . . . (pugnō, pugnās, pugnat)
  c Fēlīx est lībertus; Fēlīx cum Caeciliō . . . . (cēnō, cēnās, cēnat)
  d ego multōs spectātōrēs in amphitheātrō . . . . (videō, vidēs, videt)
  e tū in vīllā magnificā . . . . (habitō, habitās, habitat)
  f Rēgulus hodiē diem nātālem . . . . (celebrō, celebrās, celebrat)
  g tū saepe ad amphitheātrum . . . . (veniō, venīs, venit)
  h ego rem . . . . (intellegō, intellegis, intellegit)

3 Translate this story:

Lūcia et fēlēs

Lūcia et Melissa per viam dēsertam ambulābant. subitō
magnum clāmōrem audīvērunt et lībertum ingentem
cōnspexērunt. lībertus erat ēbrius. fēlem tenēbat et
vehementer eam pulsābat. fēlēs perterrita ululābat. Lūcia,
postquam hoc vīdit, statim ad lībertum cucurrit.   5
    "pestis! dēsiste!" clāmāvit.
    lībertus attonitus Lūciam spectāvit.
    "tū es puella stultissima," inquit. "nēmō mē impūne vexat."
    tum lībertus fēlem ad terram coniēcit et Lūciam
ferōciter petīvit. fēlēs fūgit, sed Lūcia immōta stābat.   10
    "manē ubi es!" inquit. "in magnō perīculō es. ego
morbum mortiferum habeō. heri duo fūrēs, postquam mē
tetigērunt, celeriter exspīrāvērunt. omnēs hominēs hunc
morbum valdē timent."
    lībertus, postquam hoc audīvit, perterritus fūgit.   15
    Melissa sollicita erat.
    "Lūcia," inquit, "morbum mortiferum habēs?"
    Lūcia rīsit.
    "minimē!" inquit. "nūllum morbum habeō. lībertus
ingēns est, sed stultissimus."   20

eam	*it*
dēsiste!	*stop!*
stultissima	*very stupid*
impūne	*safely*
coniēcit	*hurled, threw*
fūgit	*fled*
manē!	*stay!*
immōta	*still, motionless*
perīculō	*danger*
morbum	*illness*
mortiferum	*deadly*
tetigērunt	*touched*
exspīrāvērunt	*died*
rīsit	*laughed*
minimē!	*no!*

Gladiatorial shows

Among the most popular entertainments in all parts of the Roman world were shows in which gladiators fought each other. These contests were usually held in an amphitheater. This was a large oval building, without a roof, in which rising tiers of seats surrounded an arena. Canvas awnings, supported by ropes and pulleys, were spread over part of the seating area to give shelter from the sun. The amphitheater at Pompeii was large enough to contain the whole population as well as many visitors from nearby towns. Spectators paid no admission fee, as the shows were given by wealthy individuals at their own expense.

Among the many advertisements for gladiatorial shows that are to be seen painted on the walls of buildings is this one:

> **Twenty pairs of gladiators, given by Lucretius Satrius Valens, priest of Nero, and ten pairs of gladiators provided by his son will fight at Pompeii from 8 to 12 April. There will also be an animal hunt. Awnings will be provided.**

Soon after dawn on the day of a show, the spectators would begin to take their places. As in the theater, it is unclear whether women sat apart from men. A trumpet blared and priests came out to perform the religious ceremony with which the games began. Then the gladiators entered in procession, paraded round the arena, and saluted the sponsor of the show. The gladiators were then paired off to fight each other and the contests began.

The inside of the Pompeii amphitheater as it is today, looking northwest toward Vesuvius. Compare the drawing on page 113. The building held about 20,000 people and the number of seats was being increased when the city was destroyed.

Bird's-eye view of the amphitheater showing the awning.

The gladiators were slaves, condemned criminals, prisoners of war, or free volunteers; they lived and trained in a "school" or barracks under the supervision of a professional trainer.

Part of the program of one particular show, together with details of the results, reads as follows:

A Thracian versus a Murmillo
Won: Pugnax from Nero's school: 3 times a winner
Died: Murranus from Nero's school: 3 times a winner

A Heavily armed Gladiator versus a Thracian
Won: Cycnus from the school of Julius: 8 times a winner
Allowed to live: Atticus from the school of Julius: 14 times a winner

Chariot Fighters
Won: Scylax from the school of Julius: 26 times a winner
Allowed to live: Publius Ostorius: 51 times a winner

The fight ended with the death or surrender of one of the gladiators. The illustrations below, based on a relief from the tomb of a wealthy Pompeian, show the defeated gladiator appealing to the spectators; the victor stands by ready to kill him if they decide that he deserves to die. Notice the arm raised in appeal. The spectators indicated their wishes by turning their thumbs up or down: probably turning the thumb up toward the chest meant "kill him," while turning it down meant "let him live." The final decision for death or mercy was made by the sponsor of the show. It was not unusual for the life of the loser to be spared, especially if he were a well-known gladiator with a good number of victories to his credit. The most successful gladiators were great favorites with the crowd and received gifts of money from their admirers. One popular Pompeian gladiator was described as **suspīrium puellārum**: "the girls' heartthrob." Eventually, if a gladiator survived long enough or showed great skill and courage, he would be awarded the wooden sword. This was a high honor and meant he would not have to fight again.

Gladiators' armor

Gladiators were not all armed in the same way. Some, who were known as Samnites, carried an oblong shield and a short sword; others, known as Thracians, had a round shield and a curved sword or dagger. Another type of gladiator armed with sword and shield wore a helmet with a crest shaped like a fish; the Greek name for the fish was "mormillos" and the gladiator was known as a **murmillō**. *The murmillones were often matched against the* **rētiāriī** *who were armed with* **rētia** *(nets) and three-pronged tridents.*

Other types of gladiator fought with spears, on horseback, or from chariots. Occasionally women gladiators were used, bringing additional variety to the show.

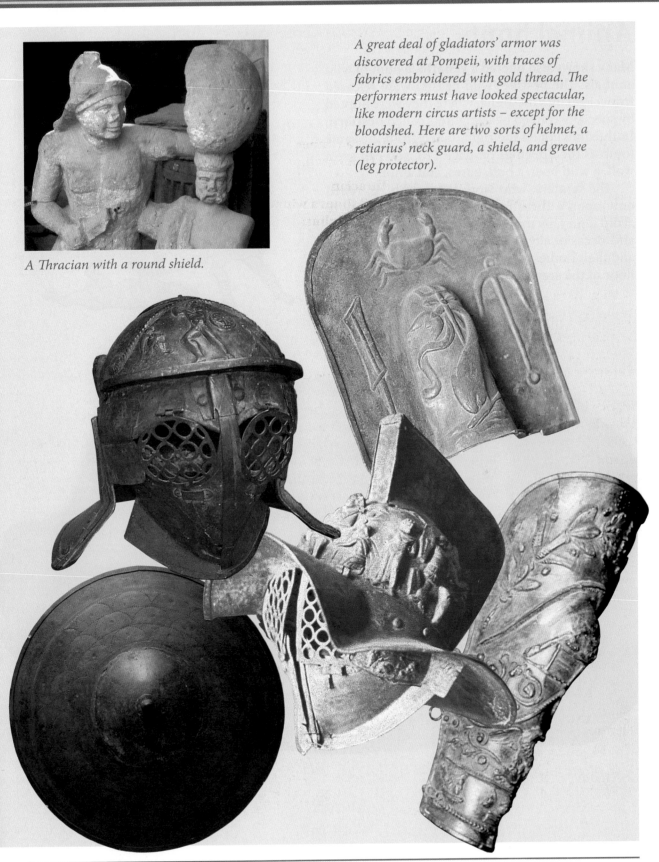

A great deal of gladiators' armor was discovered at Pompeii, with traces of fabrics embroidered with gold thread. The performers must have looked spectacular, like modern circus artists – except for the bloodshed. Here are two sorts of helmet, a retiarius' neck guard, a shield, and greave (leg protector).

A Thracian with a round shield.

Animal hunts

Many shows also offered a **vēnātiō**, a hunt of wild animals. The **bēstiae** (wild beasts) were released from cages into the arena, where they were hunted by specially trained beast fighters called **bēstiāriī**. In the drawing on the right, taken from the same tomb as the drawings on page 110, you can see a wolf, a wild boar, a bull, hares, and a lion.

The hunters, who wore light clothing, relied only upon a thrusting spear and their agility to avoid injury. By the end of the hunt all the animals and occasionally a few hunters had been killed, and their bodies were dragged out from the sandy floor of the arena to be disposed of.

The riot at Pompeii

The story told in this Stage is based on an actual event which occurred in AD 59. In addition to the evidence given in the wall painting above, the event is also described by the Roman historian Tacitus in these words:

About this time, a slight incident led to a serious outburst of rioting between the people of Pompeii and Nuceria. It occurred at a show of gladiators, sponsored by Livineius Regulus. While hurling insults at each other, in the usual manner of country people, they suddenly began to throw stones as well. Finally, they drew swords and attacked each other. The men of Pompeii won the fight. As a result, most of the families of Nuceria lost a father or a son. Many of the wounded were taken to Rome, where the Emperor Nero requested the senate to hold an inquiry. After the inquiry, the senate forbade the Pompeians to hold such shows for ten years. Livineius and others who had encouraged the riot were sent into exile.

This drawing of a gladiator with the palm of victory was scratched on a wall, with a message that may refer to the riot and its aftermath: "Campanians, in your moment of victory you perished along with the Nucerians."

Vocabulary checklist 8

agitat: agitāvit	chases, hunts
cōnsūmit: cōnsūmpsit	eats
dūcit: dūxit	leads, takes
eum	him
facile	easily
ferōx	fierce
gladius	sword
hic	this
ignāvus	cowardly
nūntius	messenger
pēs	foot
porta	gate
postulat: postulāvit	demands
puer	boy
pugnat: pugnāvit	fights
saepe	often
sanguis	blood
silva	woods, forest
spectāculum	show, spectacle
statim	at once
tōtus	whole

A retiarius who lost his fight. The symbol beside his trident is θ (theta), the first letter of the Greek word for death (thanatos).

THERMAE

Stage 9

1   Quīntus ad thermās vēnit.

2   Quīntus servō pecūniam dedit.

3   amīcī Quīntum laetē salūtāvērunt, quod diem nātālem celebrābat.

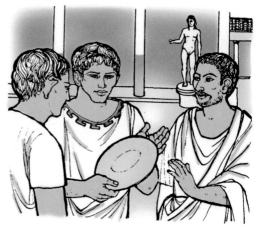

4   Quīntus discum novum ferēbat. Quīntus amīcīs discum ostendit.

5   postquam Quīntus discum ēmīsit, discus statuam percussit.

6   ēheu! statua nāsum frāctum habēbat.

7 Metella et Melissa in forō ambulābant.
   Metella fīliō dōnum quaerēbat.

8 fēminae mercātōrem cōnspexērunt.
   mercātor fēminīs togās ostendit.

9 Metella Quīntō togam ēlēgit. Melissa
   mercātōrī pecūniam dedit.

10 Grumiō cēnam optimam in culīnā
   parābat. coquus Quīntō cēnam parābat,
   quod diem nātālem celebrābat.

11 multī hospitēs cum Quīntō cēnābant.
   Clēmēns hospitibus vīnum offerēbat.

12 ancilla triclīnium intrāvit. Quīntus ancillae
   signum dedit. ancilla suāviter cantāvit.

in palaestrā

When you have read this story, answer the questions opposite.

Caecilius Quīntō discum dedit, quod diem nātālem celebrābat.
tum Caecilius fīlium ad thermās dūxit, ubi palaestra erat. servus
Quīntō discum ferēbat.

Caecilius et fīlius, postquam thermās intrāvērunt, ad
palaestram contendērunt. turba ingēns in palaestrā erat. Quīntus   5
multōs iuvenēs et āthlētās cōnspexit. Quīntus multās statuās in
palaestrā vīdit.

"Pompēiānī āthlētīs nōtissimīs statuās posuērunt," inquit
Caecilius.

in palaestrā erat porticus ingēns. spectātōrēs in porticū   10
stābant. servī spectātōribus vīnum offerēbant.

Quīntus turbam prope porticum vīdit. āthlēta ingēns in
mediā turbā stābat.

"quis est āthlēta ille?" rogāvit Quīntus.

"ille est Milō, āthlēta nōtissimus," respondit Caecilius.   15
Caecilius et Quīntus ad Milōnem contendērunt.

Quīntus āthlētae discum novum ostendit. Milō, postquam
discum īnspexit, ad mediam palaestram prōcessit. āthlēta
palaestram circumspectāvit et discum ēmīsit. discus longē per
aurās ēvolāvit. spectātōrēs āthlētam laudāvērunt. servus Milōnī   20
discum quaesīvit. servus, postquam discum invēnit, ad
Milōnem rediit. servus āthlētae discum offerēbat. āthlēta tamen
discum nōn accēpit.

"discus nōn est meus," inquit Milō.

servus Quīntō discum trādidit. tum iuvenis quoque discum   25
ēmīsit. discus iterum per aurās ēvolāvit. discus tamen statuam
percussit.

"ēheu!" clāmāvit Caecilius. "statua nāsum frāctum habet."

Quīntus rīdēbat. Pompēiānī rīdēbant. Milō tamen nōn
rīdēbat.   30

"cūr tū nōn rīdēs?" rogāvit iuvenis.

Milō erat īrātissimus.

"pestis!" respondit āthlēta. "mea est statua!"

in palaestrā *in the palaestra, in the exercise area*

discum *discus*
thermās *baths*
ferēbat *was carrying*

āthlētās *athletes*
statuās *statues*
posuērunt *have put up*

porticus *colonnade*
offerēbant *were offering*

in mediā turbā *in the middle of the crowd*
āthlēta ille *that athlete*

novum *new*

longē *a long way, far*
per aurās ēvolāvit *flew through the air*
invēnit *found*
rediit *went back*
nōn accēpit *did not accept*
trādidit *handed over*

nāsum frāctum *a broken nose*

Questions

1 Why did Caecilius give Quintus a discus?
2 Why do you think Caecilius took Quintus to the baths (lines 1–2)?
3 **turba ingēns in palaestrā erat** (line 5). Who were in the crowd?
4 Why were there statues in the palaestra?
5 Pick out two Latin words used in lines 12–15 to describe the athlete Milo. What do they tell us about him?
6 **āthlēta palaestram circumspectāvit** (lines 18–19). Why do you think Milo did this before throwing the discus?
7 How did the spectators react in line 20? Why did they react in this way?
8 **discus nōn est meus** (line 24). What had just happened to make Milo say this?
9 In lines 26–28, what happened when Quintus threw the discus?
10 How was Milo's reaction different from that of the Pompeians (lines 29–33)? Do you think he was right to behave as he did?

The palaestra of the Stabian Baths at Pompeii.

About the language

1   Study the following examples:

Clēmēns **puellae** vīnum offerēbat.
*Clemens was offering wine **to the girl**.*

iuvenis **servō** pecūniam trādidit.
*The young man handed over money **to the slave**.*

dominus **mercātōrī** statuam ēmit.
*The master bought a statue **for the merchant**.*

Grumiō **ancillīs** cēnam parāvit.
*Grumio prepared a dinner **for the slave girls**.*

Quīntus **amīcīs** discum ostendit.
*Quintus showed the discus **to his friends**.*

servī **leōnibus** cibum dedērunt.
*The slaves gave food **to the lions**.*

The Latin words in **boldface** are nouns in the **dative case**.

2   You have now met three cases. Notice the different ways in which
they are used:

nominative   **servus** dormiēbat.
               The slave was sleeping.

dative   dominus **servō** signum dedit.
               *The master gave a sign **to the slave**.*

accusative   dominus **servum** excitāvit.
               *The master woke **the slave**.*

3 Here is a full list of the noun endings that you have met.
The new dative cases are in **boldface**.

		first declension	*second declension*	*third declension*
SINGULAR	*nominative*	puella	servus	mercātor
	dative	**puellae**	**servō**	**mercātōrī**
	accusative	puellam	servum	mercātōrem
PLURAL	*nominative*	puellae	servī	mercātōrēs
	dative	**puellīs**	**servīs**	**mercātōribus**
	accusative	puellās	servōs	mercātōrēs

4 Further examples:

a ancilla dominō cibum ostendit.
b agricola uxōrī ānulum ēmit.
c servus Metellae togam trādidit.
d mercātor gladiātōribus pecūniam offerēbat.
e fēmina ancillīs tunicās quaerēbat.

5 Notice the different cases of the words for "I" and "you":

nominative	ego	tū
dative	mihi	tibi
accusative	mē	tē

ego senem salūtō. *I greet the old man.*
senex **mihi** statuam ostendit. *The old man shows a statue to me.*
senex **mē** salūtat. *The old man greets me.*

tū pictūram pingis. *You are painting a picture.*
āthlēta **tibi** pecūniam dat. *The athlete gives money to you.*
āthlēta **tē** laudat. *The athlete praises you.*

in tabernā

Metella et Melissa ē vīllā māne discessērunt. Metella fīliō togam
quaerēbat. Metella et ancilla, postquam forum intrāvērunt,
tabernam cōnspexērunt, ubi togae optimae erant. multae
fēminae erant in tabernā. servī fēminīs stolās ostendēbant. duo
gladiātōrēs quoque in tabernā erant. servī gladiātōribus tunicās   5
ostendēbant.

    mercātor in mediā tabernā stābat. mercātor erat Marcellus.
Marcellus, postquam Metellam vīdit, rogāvit,
    "quid quaeris, domina?"
    "togam quaerō," inquit Metella. "ego fīliō dōnum quaerō,   10
quod diem nātālem celebrat."
    "ego multās togās habeō," respondit mercātor.
    mercātor servīs signum dedit. servī mercātōrī togās celeriter
trādidērunt. Marcellus fēminīs togās ostendit. Metella et ancilla
togās īnspexērunt.   15
    "hercle!" clāmāvit Melissa. "hae togae sunt sordidae."
Marcellus servōs vituperāvit.
    "sunt intus togae splendidae," inquit Marcellus.
Marcellus fēminās intus dūxit. mercātor fēminīs aliās togās
ostendit. Metella Quīntō mox togam splendidam ēlēgit.   20
    "haec toga, quantī est?" rogāvit Metella.
    "quīnquāgintā dēnāriōs cupiō," respondit Marcellus.
    "quīnquāgintā dēnāriōs cupis! furcifer!" clāmāvit Melissa.
"ego tibi decem dēnāriōs offerō."
    "quadrāgintā dēnāriōs cupiō," respondit mercātor.   25
    "tibi quīndecim dēnāriōs offerō," inquit ancilla.
    "quid? haec est toga pulcherrima! quadrāgintā dēnāriōs
cupiō," respondit Marcellus.
    "tū nimium postulās," inquit Metella. "ego tibi trīgintā
dēnāriōs dō."
    "cōnsentiō," respondit Marcellus.   30
    Melissa Marcellō pecūniam dedit.
Marcellus Metellae togam trādidit.
    "ego tibi grātiās maximās agō,
domina," inquit Marcellus.   35

māne *in the morning*
togam *toga*

domina *my lady, ma'am*
dōnum *present, gift*
hae togae *these togas*
sordidae *dirty*
intus *inside*
aliās *other*
ēlēgit *chose*
haec *this*
quantī est? *how much is it?*
quīnquāgintā dēnāriōs *fifty denarii*
cupiō *I want*
decem *ten*
quadrāgintā *forty*
quīndecim *fifteen*
pulcherrima *very beautiful*
nimium *too much*
trīgintā *thirty*
cōnsentiō *I agree*
ego tibi grātiās maximās agō *I thank you very much*

A fabric shop.

Practicing the language

1 Complete each sentence with the verb that makes good sense.
Then translate the sentence, taking care with the different forms of the noun.

> For example: mercātōrēs fēminīs tunicās . . . . (audīvērunt, ostendērunt,
> timuērunt)
> mercātōrēs fēminīs tunicās **ostendērunt**.
> *The merchants showed the tunics to the women.*

  a ancilla dominō vīnum . . . . (timuit, dedit, salūtāvit)
  b iuvenis puellae stolam . . . . (ēmit, vēnit, prōcessit)
  c fēminae servīs tunicās . . . . (intrāvērunt, quaesīvērunt, contendērunt)
  d cīvēs āctōrī pecūniam . . . . (laudāvērunt, vocāvērunt, trādidērunt)
  e centuriō mercātōribus decem dēnāriōs . . . . (trādidit, ēmit, vīdit)

2 Complete each sentence with the correct form of the verb. Then translate the sentence.

> For example: gladiātor amīcīs togam . . . . (ostendit, ostendērunt)
> gladiātor amīcīs togam **ostendit**.
> *The gladiator showed the toga to his friends.*

  a puella gladiātōribus tunicās . . . . (dedit, dedērunt)
  b cīvēs Milōnī statuam . . . . (posuit, posuērunt)
  c mercātor amīcō vīnum . . . . (trādidit, trādidērunt)
  d coquus ancillae ānulum . . . . (ēmit, ēmērunt)
  e Clēmēns et Grumiō Metellae cēnam optimam . . . . (parāvit, parāvērunt)

3 This exercise is based on the story **in tabernā**, opposite. Read the story again.
Write out each sentence, completing it with the correct noun or phrase. Then
translate the sentence.

  a Metella . . . . ad forum ambulāvit. (cum Quīntō, cum Grumiōne, cum Melissā)
  b postquam forum intrāvērunt, ... cōnspexērunt. (portum, tabernam, vīllam)
  c Metella gladiātōrēs et . . . . in tabernā vīdit. (āctōrēs, fēminās, centuriōnēs)
  d servī fēminīs . . . . ostendēbant. (tunicās, stolās, togās)
  e servī gladiātōribus . . . . ostendēbant. (togās, stolās, tunicās)
  f mercātor servīs . . . . dedit. (signum, togam, gladium)
  g servī mercātōrī . . . . trādidērunt. (togam, togās, stolās)
  h mercātor . . . . vituperāvit, quod togae erant sordidae. (gladiātōrēs, fēminās, servōs)

in apodytēriō

in apodytēriō *in the changing room*

duo servī in apodytēriō stant. servī sunt Sceledrus et Anthrāx.

Sceledrus:	cūr nōn labōrās, Anthrāx? num dormīs?
Anthrāx:	quid dīcis? dīligenter labōrō. ego cīvibus togās custōdiō.
Sceledrus:	togās custōdīs? mendāx es!
Anthrāx:	cūr mē vituperās? mendāx nōn sum. togās custōdiō.
Sceledrus:	tē vituperō, quod fūr est in apodytēriō, sed tū nihil facis.
Anthrāx:	ubi est fūr? fūrem nōn videō.
Sceledrus:	ecce! homō ille est fūr. fūrem facile agnōscō. *(Sceledrus Anthrācī fūrem ostendit. fūr togam suam dēpōnit et togam splendidam induit. servī ad fūrem statim currunt.)*
Anthrāx:	quid facis? furcifer! haec toga nōn est tua!
fūr:	mendāx es! mea est toga! abī!
Sceledrus:	tē agnōscō! pauper es, sed togam splendidam geris. *(mercātor intrat. togam frūstrā quaerit.)*
mercātor:	ēheu! ubi est toga mea? toga ēvānuit! *(mercātor circumspectat.)* ecce! hic fūr togam meam gerit!
fūr:	parce! parce! pauperrimus sum ... uxor mea est aegra ... decem līberōs habeō ...

Line numbers: 5, 10, 15, 20

num dormīs? *surely you are not asleep?*

suam *his*
induit *is putting on*

abī! *go away!*
pauper *poor*
geris *you are wearing*

parce! *have pity on me! spare me!*
pauperrimus *very poor*
aegra *sick, ill*
līberōs *children*
audiunt *listen to*

mercātor et servī fūrem nōn audiunt, sed eum ad iūdicem trahunt.

This mosaic of a squid is in an apodyterium in Herculaneum.

An apodyterium (changing room) in the women's section of the Stabian Baths at Pompeii.

The caldarium (hot room) in the Forum Baths, Pompeii. At the nearer end note the large rectangular marble bath, which was filled with hot water. At the far end there is a stone basin for cold water. Rooms in baths often had grooved, curved ceilings to channel condensation down the walls.

The baths

About the middle of the afternoon, Caecilius would make his way, with a group of friends, to the public baths. The great majority of Pompeians did not have bathrooms in their houses, so they went regularly to the public baths to keep themselves clean. As at a leisure center, city pool, or health club today, they could also take exercise, meet friends, and have a snack. Let us imagine that Caecilius decides to visit the baths situated just to the north of the forum, and let us follow him through the various rooms and activities.

At one of the entrances, he pays a small admission fee to the doorkeeper and then goes to the **palaestra** (exercise area). This is an open space surrounded by a colonnade, rather like a large peristylium. Here he spends a little time greeting other friends and taking part in some of the popular exercises, which included throwing a large ball from one to another, wrestling, and fencing with wooden swords. These games were not taken too seriously but were a pleasant preparation for the bath which followed.

From the palaestra, Caecilius and his friends walk along a passage into a large hall known as the **apodytērium** (changing room). Here they undress and hand their clothes to one of the slave attendants who places them in recesses arranged in rows along the wall.

Leaving the apodyterium, they pass through an arched doorway into the **tepidārium** (warm room) and spend a little time sitting on benches round the wall in a warm, steamy atmosphere, perspiring gently and preparing for the higher temperatures in the next room.

This is the **caldārium** (hot room). At one end of the caldarium there was a large marble bath, rectangular in shape, and stretching across the full width of the room. This bath was filled with hot water in which the bathers sat or wallowed. The Romans did not have soap, but used olive oil instead. After soaking in the bath, Caecilius summons a slave to rub him down with the oil that he has brought with him in a little pot. For this rubbing down, Caecilius lies on a marble slab while the slave works the oil into his skin, and then gently removes it and the dirt with a blunt metal scraper known as a **strigil**. Next comes the masseur to massage skin and muscles. Refreshed by this treatment, Caecilius then goes to the large stone basin at the other end of the caldarium for a rinse down with cold water.

Strigils and oil bottles.

1 *The entrance hall with the apodyterium beyond.*
Stabian Baths, Pompeii.

2 *The tepidarium. This sometimes had recesses for clothes like the apodyterium.*
Forum Baths, Pompeii.

3 *The hot tub in the caldarium.*
Herculaneum.

4 *The caldarium, showing a marble bench for sitting or massage.*
Herculaneum.

5 *The frigidarium: cold plunge bath.*
Forum Baths, Pompeii.

Before dressing again he might well visit the **frigidārium** (cold room) and there take a plunge in a deep circular pool of unheated water, followed by a brisk rub down with his towel.

Metella, too, would have visited public baths. Some baths had a separate suite of rooms for the use of female bathers; others may have given access to men and women at different times, or may have allowed mixed bathing. We do not know whether women were allowed to exercise in the palaestra. In the Forum and Stabian Baths, where separate facilities for men and women existed, those for the women were smaller, and had a pool of cold water in the apodyterium rather than a separate frigidarium. The smaller facilities may be an indication that fewer women attended the baths, or that women attended less regularly than men. Alternatively, it may indicate that women's needs were regarded as less important than those of men.

A visit to the baths was a leisurely social occasion. Men and women enjoyed a noisy, relaxed time in the company of friends. The Roman writer Seneca lived uncomfortably close to a set of baths in Rome and his description gives us a vivid impression of the atmosphere there:

I am surrounded by uproar. I live over a set of baths. Just imagine the babel of sounds that strikes my ears. When the athletic gentlemen below are exercising themselves, lifting lead weights, I can hear their grunts. I can hear the whistling of their breath as it escapes from their lungs. I can hear somebody enjoying a cheap rub down and the smack of the masseur's hands on his shoulders. If his hand comes down flat, it makes one sound; if it comes down hollowed, it makes another. Add to this the noise of a brawler or thief being arrested down below, the racket made by the man who likes to sing in his bath, or the sound of enthusiasts who hurl themselves into the water with a tremendous splash. Next I can hear the screech of the hair plucker, who advertises himself by shouting. He is never quiet except when he is plucking hair and making his victim shout instead. Finally, just imagine the cries of the cake seller, the sausage man, and the other food sellers as they advertise their goods round the bath, all adding to the din.

A bronze statue of a boxer from a set of baths in Rome. His training would no doubt have contributed to the din about which Seneca complains.

Heating the baths

The Romans were not the first people to build public baths. This was one of the many things they learned from the Greeks. But with their engineering skill the Romans greatly improved the methods of heating them. The previous method had been to heat the water in tanks over a furnace and to stand braziers (portable metal containers in which wood was burned) in the tepidarium and the caldarium to keep up the air temperature. The braziers were not very efficient and they failed to heat the floor.

In the first century BC, a Roman invented the first central heating system. The furnace was placed below the floor level; the floor was supported on small brick piles leaving space through which hot air from the furnace could circulate. In this way, the floor was warmed from below. The hot bath was placed near the furnace and a steady temperature was maintained by the hot air passing immediately below. Later, flues (channels) were built into the walls and warm air from beneath the floor was drawn up through them. This ingenious heating system was known as a **hypocaust**. It was used not only in baths but also in private houses, particularly in the colder parts of the Roman empire. Many examples have been found in Britain. Wood was the fuel most commonly burned in the furnaces.

Hypocaust in the Stabian Baths. Notice the floor suspended on brick piles, so that hot air can circulate beneath and warm both the room and the tank of water for bathing.

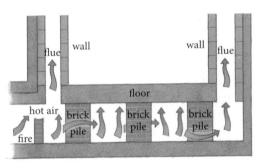

A hypocaust viewed from the side.

Plan of the Forum Baths, Pompeii

The men's section is outlined in black and the women's in blue. See how the hottest rooms (red) in both suites are arranged on either side of the one furnace (marked by an orange dot). The blue circles near this are boilers. After losing some heat to the hot rooms the hot air goes on to warm the warm rooms (pink).

Key:
P: palaestra
A: apodytērium
T: tepidārium
C: caldārium
F: frigidārium

The small arrows mark public entrances.
The orange spaces are shops.

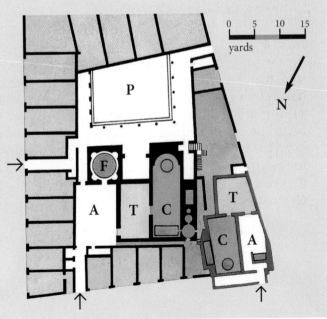

Vocabulary checklist 9

agnōscit: agnōvit	*recognizes*
celeriter	*quickly*
cupit: cupīvit	*wants*
dat: dedit	*gives*
diēs	*day*
ēmittit: ēmīsit	*throws, sends out*
fert: tulit	*brings, carries*
homō	*human being, man*
hospes	*guest*
ille	*that*
īnspicit: īnspexit	*looks at, examines*
iterum	*again*
manet: mānsit	*remains, stays*
medius	*middle*
mox	*soon*
offert: obtulit	*offers*
ostendit: ostendit	*shows*
post	*after*
prōcēdit: prōcessit	*advances, proceeds*
pulcher	*beautiful*
revenit: revēnit	*comes back, returns*
trādit: trādidit	*hands over*

The floors of baths often had marine themes. This mosaic of an octopus is in the women's baths at Herculaneum.

RHETOR

Stage 10

1 Rōmānus dīcit,
"nōs Rōmānī sumus architectī. nōs viās et pontēs aedificāmus."

2 "nōs Rōmānī sumus agricolae. nōs fundōs optimōs habēmus."

3   Graecus dīcit,
     "nōs Graecī sumus sculptōrēs. nōs statuās pulchrās facimus."

4   "nōs Graecī sumus pictōrēs. nōs pictūrās pingimus."

5   Rōmānus dīcit,
"vōs Graecī estis ignāvī. vōs āctōrēs semper spectātis."

6   Graecus dīcit,
"vōs Rōmānī estis barbarī. vōs semper pugnātis."

7 Rōmānus dīcit,
  "nōs sumus callidī. nōs rēs ūtilēs facimus."

8 Graecus dīcit,
  "nōs sumus callidiōrēs quam vōs. nōs Graecī Rōmānōs docēmus."

contrōversia

contrōversia *debate*

Quīntus amīcum Graecum habēbat. amīcus erat Alexander.
Quīntus et Alexander ad palaestram ībant, ubi rhētor Graecus
erat. hic rhētor erat Theodōrus et prope palaestram habitābat. in
palaestrā erat porticus longa, ubi Theodōrus iuvenēs docēbat.
postquam ad hanc porticum vēnērunt, Alexander et Quīntus   5
rhētorem audīvērunt. rhētor iuvenibus contrōversiam
nūntiābat, "Graecī sunt meliōrēs quam Rōmānī."

ībant *were going*
rhētor *teacher*
longa *long*
docēbat *used to teach*
hanc *this*
meliōrēs quam *better than*

Quīntus vehementer exclāmāvit,
    "minimē! nōs Rōmānī sumus meliōrēs quam Graecī."
Theodōrus, postquam hanc sententiam audīvit, respondit,   10
    "haec est tua sententia. nōs tamen nōn sententiam quaerimus,
nōs argūmentum quaerimus." tum Quīntus rhētorī et amīcīs
argūmentum explicāvit.
    "nōs Rōmānī sumus fortissimī. nōs barbarōs ferōcissimōs
superāmus. nōs imperium maximum habēmus. nōs pācem   15
servāmus. vōs Graecī semper contentiōnēs habētis. vōs semper
estis turbulentī.
    "nōs sumus architectī optimī. nōs viās et pontēs ubīque
aedificāmus. urbs Rōma est maior quam omnēs urbēs.
    "postrēmō nōs Rōmānī dīligenter labōrāmus. deī igitur nōbīs   20
imperium maximum dant. vōs Graecī estis ignāvī. vōs
numquam labōrātis. deī vōbīs nihil dant."

sententiam *opinion*
argūmentum *proof*
barbarōs *barbarians*
imperium *empire*
pācem *peace*
servāmus *keep, preserve*
architectī *builders, architects*
pontēs *bridges*
ubīque *everywhere*
aedificāmus *build*
maior quam *greater than, bigger than*
postrēmō *lastly*
deī *gods*
dant *give*
ignāvī *lazy*

The Romans built this bridge at Alcantara in Spain.

postquam Quīntus hanc sententiam explicāvit, iuvenēs
Pompēiānī vehementer plausērunt et eum laudāvērunt. deinde
Alexander surrēxit. iuvenēs Pompēiānī tacuērunt et 25
Alexandrum intentē spectāvērunt.

"vōs Rōmānī estis miserandī. vōs imperium maximum
habētis, sed vōs estis imitātōrēs; nōs Graecī sumus auctōrēs. vōs
Graecās statuās spectātis, vōs Graecōs librōs legitis, Graecōs
rhētorēs audītis. vōs Rōmānī estis rīdiculī, quod estis Graeciōrēs 30
quam nōs Graecī!"

iuvenēs, postquam Alexander sententiam suam explicāvit,
rīsērunt. tum Theodōrus nūntiāvit,
"Alexander victor est. argūmentum optimum explicāvit."

deinde *then*
surrēxit *got up*

miserandī *pathetic, pitiful*
imitātōrēs *imitators*
auctōrēs *creators*
librōs *books*

Greek writers and thinkers have influenced people's minds to this day; far left: the tragic dramatist Euripides; left: the philosopher Anaximander who taught that the universe was governed by law. He is holding a sundial, which he is said to have invented.

About the language 1

1 In this Stage, you have met sentences with "we" and "you":

nōs labōrāmus.	*We work.*	vōs labōrātis.	*You work.*
nōs currimus.	*We run.*	vōs curritis.	*You run.*

Notice that **vōs labōrātis** and **vōs curritis** are **plural** forms.
They are used when "you" refers to more than one person.

2 You have now met the whole of the present tense:

(ego)	portō	*I carry, I am carrying*
(tū)	portās	*you (singular) carry, you are carrying*
	portat	*s/he carries, s/he is carrying*
(nōs)	portāmus	*we carry, we are carrying*
(vōs)	portātis	*you (plural) carry, you are carrying*
	portant	*they carry, they are carrying*

3 Notice that **nōs** and **vōs** are not strictly necessary, since the endings -**mus** and -**tis** make it clear that "we" and "you" are being spoken about. The Romans generally used **nōs** and **vōs** only for emphasis.

4 Further examples:

   a nōs pugnāmus. vōs dormītis.
   b vōs clāmātis. nōs audīmus.
   c ambulāmus. dīcimus. vidēmus.
   d vidētis. nūntiātis. intrāmus.

5 The Latin for "we are" and "you (plural) are" is as follows:

nōs sumus iuvenēs.	*We are young men.*	**vōs estis** pictōrēs.	*You are painters.*
nōs sumus fortēs.	*We are brave.*	**vōs estis** ignāvī.	*You are lazy.*

So the complete present tense of **sum** is:

(ego)	sum	*I am*
(tū)	es	*you (singular) are*
	est	*s/he is*
(nōs)	sumus	*we are*
(vōs)	estis	*you (plural) are*
	sunt	*they are*

statuae

postquam Theodōrus Alexandrum laudāvit, iuvenēs Pompēiānī
ē porticū discessērunt. Alexander et Quīntus ad vīllam
ambulābant, ubi Alexander et duo frātrēs habitābant.

    Alexander frātribus dōnum quaerēbat, quod diem nātālem
celebrābant.

    in viā īnstitor parvās statuās vēndēbat et clāmābat:

    "statuae! optimae statuae!"

    Alexander frātribus statuās ēmit. statuae erant senex, iuvenis,
puella pulchra. Alexander, postquam statuās ēmit, ad vīllam
cum Quīntō contendit.

    duo frātrēs in hortō sedēbant. Diodōrus pictūram pingēbat,
Thrasymachus librum Graecum legēbat. postquam Alexander et
Quīntus vīllam intrāvērunt, puerī ad eōs cucurrērunt. Diodōrus
statuās cōnspexit.

    "Alexander, quid portās?" inquit.

    "vōs estis fēlīcēs," inquit Alexander. "ego vōbīs dōnum habeō
quod vōs diem nātālem celebrātis. ecce!" Alexander frātribus
statuās ostendit.

    "quam pulchra est puella!" inquit Diodōrus. "dā mihi
puellam!"

    "minimē! frāter, dā mihi puellam!" clāmāvit Thrasymachus.

    puerī dissentiēbant et lacrimābant.

    "hercle! vōs estis stultissimī puerī!" clāmāvit Alexander īrātus.
"semper dissentītis, semper lacrimātis. abīte! abīte! ego statuās
retineō!"

    puerī, postquam Alexander hoc dīxit, abiērunt. Diodōrus
pictūram in terram dēiēcit, quod īrātus erat. Thrasymachus
librum in piscīnam dēiēcit, quod īrātissimus erat.

    tum Quīntus dīxit,

    "Alexander, dā mihi statuās! Thrasymache! Diodōre! venīte
hūc! Thrasymache, ecce! ego tibi senem dō, quod senex erat
philosophus. Diodōre, tibi iuvenem dō, quod iuvenis erat pictor.
ego mihi puellam dō, quod ego sum sōlus! vōsne estis contentī?"

    "sumus contentī," respondērunt puerī.

    "ecce, Alexander," inquit Quīntus, "vōs Graeculī estis optimī
artificēs sed turbulentī. nōs Rōmānī vōbīs pācem damus."

    "et vōs praemium accipitis," susurrāvit Thrasymachus.

frātrēs	brothers
īnstitor	street vendor
ad eōs	to them
fēlīcēs	lucky
quam!	how!
dā!	give!
dissentiēbant	were arguing
abīte!	go away!
retineō	am keeping
abiērunt	went away
in terram	onto the ground
dēiēcit	threw
in piscīnam	into the fishpond
venīte hūc!	come here!
philosophus	philosopher
pictor	painter
sōlus	lonely
vōsne estis contentī?	are you satisfied?
Graeculī	poor Greeks
praemium	profit, reward
susurrāvit	whispered, muttered

line numbers: 5, 10, 15, 20, 25, 30, 35

statuae

About the language 2

1 Study the following pairs of sentences:

nōs Rōmānī sumus callidī.
We Romans are clever.

nōs Rōmānī sumus **callidiōrēs** quam vōs Graecī.
*We Romans are **cleverer** than you Greeks.*

nōs Rōmānī sumus fortēs.
We Romans are brave.

nōs Rōmānī sumus **fortiōrēs** quam vōs Graecī.
*We Romans are **braver** than you Greeks.*

The words in **boldface** are known as **comparatives**. They are used to compare two things or groups with each other. In the examples above, the Romans are comparing themselves with the Greeks.

2 Further examples:

a Pompēiānī sunt stultī. Nūcerīnī sunt stultiōrēs quam Pompēiānī.
b Diodōrus erat īrātus, sed Thrasymachus erat īrātior quam Diodōrus.
c mea vīlla est pulchra, sed tua vīlla est pulchrior quam mea.

3 The word **magnus** forms its comparative in an unusual way:

Nūceria est magna.   Rōma est maior quam Nūceria.
Nuceria is large.   *Rome is larger than Nuceria.*

ānulus Aegyptius

Aegyptius *Egyptian*

When you have read this story, answer the questions at the end.

Syphāx in tabernā sedēbat. caupō Syphācī vīnum dedit. Syphāx caupōnī ānulum trādidit.

"pecūniam nōn habeō," inquit, "quod Neptūnus nāvem meam dēlēvit."

caupō, postquam ānulum accēpit, eum īnspexit.   5

"ānulus antīquus est," inquit.

"ita vērō, antīquus est," Syphāx caupōnī respondit. "servus

caupō *innkeeper*

Neptūnus *Neptune (god of the sea)*

dēlēvit *has destroyed*
eum *it*
antīquus *old, ancient*

Aegyptius mihi ānulum dedit. servus in pȳramide ānulum invēnit."

caupō, postquam tabernam clausit, ad vīllam suam festīnāvit. caupō uxōrī ānulum ostendit. caupō uxōrī ānulum dedit, quod ānulus eam dēlectāvit.

uxor postrīdiē ad urbem contendēbat. subitō servus ingēns in viā appāruit. pecūniam postulāvit. fēmina, quod erat perterrita, servō pecūniam dedit. servus ānulum cōnspexit. ānulum postulāvit. fēmina servō eum trādidit.

fēmina ad tabernam rediit et marītum quaesīvit. mox eum invēnit. caupō incendium spectābat. ēheu! taberna ardēbat! fēmina marītō rem tōtam nārrāvit.

"ānulus īnfēlīx est," inquit caupō. "ānulus tabernam meam dēlēvit."

servus ingēns, postquam pecūniam et ānulum cēpit, ad urbem contendit. subitō trēs servōs cōnspexit. servī inimīcī erant. inimīcī, postquam pecūniam cōnspexērunt, servum verberābant. servus fūgit, sed ānulum āmīsit.

Grumiō cum Poppaeā ambulābat. ānulum in viā invēnit.

"quid vidēs?" rogāvit Poppaea.

"ānulum videō," inquit. "ānulus Aegyptius est."

"euge!" inquit Poppaea. "ānulus fēlīx est."

in pȳramide *in a pyramid*
clausit *closed*
eam *her*
postrīdiē *on the next day*
marītum *husband*
incendium *blaze, fire*
ardēbat *was on fire*
īnfēlīx *unlucky*
āmīsit *lost*

Questions

1 How did Syphax pay for his drink?
2 Why did he pay in this way?
3 What do you think he meant in lines 3 and 4 by saying **Neptūnus nāvem meam dēlēvit**?
4 In lines 7–9, Syphax gives three pieces of information about the ring. What are they?
5 What did the innkeeper do with the ring when he returned home?
6 **uxor postrīdiē ad urbem contendēbat** (line 13). Who met the wife? What two things did he make her do?
7 What did she find when she returned to the inn (line 18)?
8 What three things happened after the huge slave met the other slaves and they spotted the money (lines 24–25)?
9 Who found the ring?
10 Poppaea thought the ring was lucky. Who had the opposite opinion earlier in the story? Who do you think was right? Give a reason.

Bronze ring with the heads of Egyptian gods.

Lūcia et Alexander

Lūcia et Melissa prope palaestram ambulant. Lūcia
Alexandrum videt.

Lūcia:	Melissa, ecce! iuvenis ille est Alexander.
Melissa:	quis est Alexander?
Lūcia:	Alexander est iuvenis Graecus. Theodōrus in 5
	palaestrā cotīdiē Alexandrum et Quīntum
	docet. Quīntus et Alexander amīcissimī sunt.
Melissa:	quam pulcher est Alexander!
Lūcia:	Alexander est callidissimus. heri Alexander
	rhētorī et amīcīs optimum argūmentum explicāvit. 10
Melissa:	Quīntus quoque callidus est.
Lūcia:	Alexander est callidior quam Quīntus. nōs Rōmānī
	nōn semper sumus meliōrēs quam Graecī.
Melissa:	Alexander tē dēlectat?
Lūcia:	minimē! quam rīdicula es, Melissa! 15
	(Lūcia ērubēscit.)

docet *teaches*
amīcissimī *very friendly,*
very good friends
callidissimus *very clever*

callidior *cleverer*

ērubēscit *blushes*

Practicing the language

1 Complete each sentence with the most suitable phrase from the box below.
Then translate the sentence.

> fābulam agimus   contrōversiam habēmus   cibum offerimus
> stolās compōnimus   pānem parāmus

a nōs sumus rhētorēs Graecī; nōs in palaestrā . . . .
b nōs sumus āctōrēs nōtissimī; nōs in theātrō . . . .
c nōs sumus ancillae pulchrae; nōs fēminīs . . . .
d nōs sumus coquī; nōs dominīs . . . .
e nōs sumus pistōrēs; nōs cīvibus . . . .

2 Complete each sentence with the most suitable noun from the box below. Then
translate the sentence.

> servī   āthlētae   pictōrēs   vēnālīciī   gladiātōrēs

a vōs estis . . . . callidī; vōs pictūrās magnificās pingitis.
b vōs estis . . . . fortēs; vōs in arēnā pugnātis.
c nōs sumus . . . .; nōs in thermīs togās custōdīmus.
d vōs servōs in forō vēnditis, quod vōs estis . . . .
e nōs ad palaestram contendimus, quod nōs sumus . . . .

Schools

The first stage of education

Quintus, and perhaps Lucia, would first have gone to school when they were about seven years old. Like other Roman schools, the one that Quintus and Lucia attended would have been small and consisted of about thirty pupils and a teacher known as the **ludī magister**. All the teaching would take place in a rented room or perhaps in a public colonnade or square, where there would be constant noise and distractions.

On the journey between home and school, pupils were normally escorted by a slave known as a **paedagōgus** who was responsible for their behavior and protection. Another slave carried their books and writing materials.

At the school of the ludi magister, pupils learned only to read and write Latin and Greek and perhaps to do simple arithmetic. Quintus and Lucia, like many children of wealthy families, would already be able to speak some Greek, which they had picked up from Greek slaves at home or friends like Alexander in the story.

Parents were not obliged by law to send their children to school, and those who wanted education for their children had to pay for it. The charges were not high and the advantages of being able to read and write were so widely appreciated that many people were prepared to pay for their sons, and perhaps their daughters too, to go to school at least for a few years.

Writing materials

The materials that Quintus and Lucia used for writing were rather different from ours. Frequently they wrote on **tabulae** (wooden tablets) coated with a thin film of wax; and they inscribed the letters on the wax surface with a thin stick of metal, bone, or ivory. This stick was called a **stilus**. The end opposite the writing point was flat so that it could be used to rub out mistakes and make the wax smooth again. Several tablets were strung together to make a little writing book. At other times they wrote with ink on papyrus, a material that looked rather like modern paper but was rougher in texture. It was manufactured from the fibers of the papyrus reed that grew along the banks of the river Nile in Egypt. For writing on papyrus they used either a reed or a goose quill sharpened and split at one end like the modern pen nib.

tabulae and stili.

Papyrus rolls, a double inkwell (for red and black ink), and a quill pen. From a Pompeian painting.

A wax tablet with a schoolboy's exercise in Greek. The master has written the top two lines and the child has copied them below.

Ink was made from soot and resin or other gummy substances, forming a paste that was thinned by adding water. The best inks were so hard and durable that they are perfectly legible even today on the pieces of papyrus that have survived.

Pictures of scenes in school show that there were generally no desks and no blackboard. Pupils sat on benches or stools, resting tablets on their knees.

Two boys and their teacher at school. The boys are using papyrus rolls.

The master sat on a high chair overlooking his class. Discipline was usually strict and sometimes harsh.

The school day began early and lasted for six hours with a short break at midday. Holidays were given on public festivals and on every ninth day which was a market day; during the hot summer months fewer pupils attended lessons, and some schoolmasters may have closed their schools altogether from July to October.

The second stage

Many children would have finished their schooling at the age of eleven, but a boy like Quintus, from a wealthy family, would have moved to a more advanced school run by a **grammaticus**. The grammaticus introduced his pupils to the work of famous Greek and Roman writers, beginning with the *Iliad* and *Odyssey* of Homer. Then the pupils moved on to the famous Greek tragedies which had been first performed in Athens in the fifth century BC. The Roman poets most frequently read at schools were Virgil and Horace. Besides reading works of literature aloud, the pupils had to analyze the grammar and learn long passages by heart; many educated people could remember these passages in later life and quote or recite them. The pupils were also taught a little history and geography, mainly in order to understand references to famous people and places mentioned in the literature.

This roughly sketched painting shows a school in session in the colonnade of the forum at Pompeii. On the right a boy is supported on another's back, for a beating.

When he left the grammaticus at the age of fifteen or sixteen, Quintus would have a very good knowledge of Greek as well as Latin. This knowledge of Greek not only introduced the pupils to a culture which the Romans greatly admired and which had inspired much of their own civilization, but was also very useful in later life because Greek was widely spoken in the countries of the eastern Mediterranean where Roman merchants and government officials frequently traveled on business.

The third stage

A few students then proceeded to the school of a **rhētor**, like Theodorus in our story. This teacher, who was often a highly educated Greek, gave more advanced lessons in literature and trained his students in the art of public speaking. This was a very important skill for young men who expected to take part in public life. For example, they needed it to present cases in the law courts, to express their opinions in council meetings, and to address the people at election time. The rhetor taught the rules for making different kinds of speeches and made his students practice arguing for and against a point of view. Students also learned how to vary their tone of voice and emphasize their words with gestures.

The poet Virgil.

Science and technical subjects

We have not so far mentioned the teaching of science and technical subjects in Roman schools. It is true that the Greeks had made important discoveries in mathematics and some aspects of physics; it is also true that the Romans were experienced in such things as the methods of surveying and the use of concrete in building. But these things played little part in school work. The purpose of ordinary Roman schools was to teach those things which were thought to be most necessary for civilized living: the ability to read and write, a knowledge of simple arithmetic, the appreciation of fine literature, and the ability to speak and argue convincingly. Science and advanced mathematics were taught to only a few students whose parents were interested and wealthy enough to pay the fees of a specialist teacher, nearly always a Greek. Technical skills were learnt by becoming an apprentice in a trade or business.

Craft skills were learned by apprenticeship. Here: carving a table leg.

Girls' education

Apart from those who went to the school of the ludi magister, many girls picked up a knowledge of reading and writing from their parents or brothers at home. Some wealthy families had an educated slave or a private tutor to teach their daughters. These girls might even have learned music, and Latin and Greek literature and philosophy, with a view to attracting a desirable husband. They also prepared for married life by learning how to supervise slaves and manage a household, which would have required at least basic arithmetic. The daughters of poorer parents learned the skills of a good housewife: cooking, cleaning, childcare, and perhaps a trade like spinning or weaving.

Vocabulary checklist 10

abit: abiit	*goes away*
accipit: accēpit	*accepts*
callidus	*clever, cunning*
contentus	*satisfied*
exclāmat: exclāmāvit	*exclaims*
frāter	*brother*
habitat: habitāvit	*lives*
imperium	*empire*
invenit: invēnit	*finds*
liber	*book*
nōs	*we*
nūntiat: nūntiāvit	*announces*
pāx	*peace*
portus	*harbor*
quam	*than*
semper	*always*
servat: servāvit	*saves, looks after*
sōlus	*alone*
suus	*his, her, their*
tacet: tacuit	*is silent, is quiet*
uxor	*wife*
vehementer	*violently, loudly*
vōs	*you (plural)*

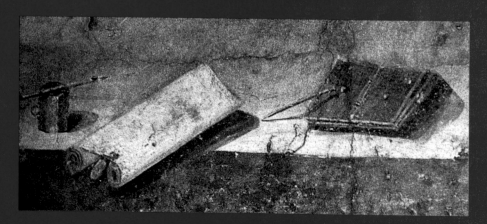

A pen (made from a reed), inkwell, papyrus roll, stilus, and wax tablets.

CANDIDATI

1 cīvēs in forō candidātōs spectant.

2 agricolae clāmant,
    "nōs candidātum optimum habēmus."
    "candidātus noster est Lūcius."
    "nōs Lūciō favēmus."

3 mercātōrēs agricolīs respondent,
    "nōs candidātum optimum habēmus."
    "candidātus noster est mercātor."
    "nōs mercātōrī favēmus."

4   pistōrēs in forō clāmant,
       "nōs pistōrēs candidātum optimum
       habēmus."
       "candidātus noster est pistor."
       "nōs pistōrī crēdimus."

5   iuvenēs pistōribus respondent,
       "nōs iuvenēs candidātum optimum
       habēmus."
       "candidātus noster est āthlēta."
       "nōs āthlētae crēdimus."

6   fūrēs clāmant,
       "nōs quoque candidātum habēmus."
       "candidātus noster est fūr."
       "nōs candidātō nostrō nōn crēdimus sed
       favēmus."

Quīntus et Lūcia

Lūcia et Quīntus in vīllā erant. Lūcia Quīntō dīxit,
  "Āfer candidātus optimus est. Āfer multās vīllās et multās
tabernās habet. Pompēiānī Āfrō favent, quod vir dīves et callidus
est."
  "minimē! Holcōnius candidātus optimus est," Quīntus sorōrī
respondit. "Holcōnius est vir nōbilis. Pompēiānī Holcōniō
crēdunt, quod pater senātor erat."
  Quīntus, quod erat īrātissimus, ē vīllā discessit. Quīntus
sibi dīxit,
  "soror mea est stultissima. gēns nostra Holcōniō semper
favet."
  Quīntus per viam ambulābat et rem cōgitābat. subitō parvam
tabernam cōnspexit, ubi scrīptor habitābat. scrīptor Sulla erat.
Quīntus, postquam tabernam vīdit, cōnsilium cēpit. tabernam
intrāvit et Sullam ad vīllam suam invītāvit.
  postquam ad vīllam vēnērunt, Quīntus Sullae mūrum
ostendit.
  "scrībe hunc titulum!" inquit. "scrībe 'Quīntus et soror
Holcōniō favent. Quīntus et soror Holcōniō crēdunt.'"
  Quīntus scrīptōrī decem dēnāriōs dedit.
  "placetne tibi?" rogāvit Quīntus.
  "mihi placet," Sulla Quīntō respondit. Sulla, postquam
dēnāriōs accēpit, titulum in mūrō scrīpsit.

5

10

15

20

candidātus *candidate*
favent *favor, give
      support to*
vir dīves *a rich man*
vir nōbilis *a man of
      noble birth*
crēdunt *trust, have faith in*
sibi dīxit *said to himself*
gēns nostra *our family*
rem cōgitābat *was
      considering the
      problem*
scrīptor *signwriter*
cōnsilium cēpit
      had an idea
mūrum *wall*
scrībe! *write!*
titulum *notice, slogan*
placetne tibi?
      *does it please you?
      does it suit you?*
scrīpsit *wrote*

Sulla

Lūcia ē vīllā vēnit. Sullam vīdit. titulum cōnspexit. postquam
titulum lēgit, īrāta erat. Lūcia scrīptōrem valdē vituperāvit.

"frāter tuus mē ad vīllam invītāvit," inquit Sulla. "frāter tuus
mihi decem dēnāriōs dedit."

"frāter meus est stultior quam asinus," Lūcia Sullae respondit.
"Sulla, ērāde illam īnscrīptiōnem! scrībe titulum novum!"

Lūcia Sullae quīndecim dēnāriōs dedit.

"placetne tibi?" rogāvit.

"mihi placet," Sulla Lūciae respondit. Sulla, postquam
īnscrīptiōnem ērāsit, hunc titulum scrīpsit, "Lūcia et frāter Āfrō
favent. Lūcia et frāter Āfrō crēdunt."

Lūcia erat laetissima et frātrem ē vīllā vocāvit. Lūcia
frātrī titulum novum ostendit. Quīntus, postquam titulum lēgit,
īrātus erat. Quīntus Lūciam vituperāvit.

"Lūcia! Quīnte! intrō īte!" clāmāvit Sulla. "cōnsilium optimum
habeō."

postquam iuvenēs vīllam intrāvērunt, Sulla celeriter rem
cōnfēcit.

duōs titulōs in mūrō scrīpsit. tum Quīntum et Lūciam ē vīllā
vocāvit.

scrīptor iuvenibus mūrum ostendit. ecce! Lūcia hunc titulum
vīdit: "Lūcia Āfrō favet. Āfer est candidātus optimus."

"euge! hic titulus mē valdē dēlectat," inquit Lūcia.

Quīntus alterum titulum in mūrō cōnspexit:
"Quīntus Holcōniō favet. Holcōnius est candidātus optimus."

Quīntus quoque laetissimus erat.

iuvenēs Sullae trīgintā dēnāriōs dedērunt. Sulla rīdēbat.
postquam Lūcia et Quīntus discessērunt, tertium titulum
addidit:

5	**asinus** *ass, donkey*
	ērāde! *rub out!*
	erase!
	illam *that*
10	**īnscrīptiōnem**
	writing
	ērāsit *rubbed out,*
	erased
15	**intrō īte!** *go inside!*
	rem cōnfēcit
	finished the job
20	
25	
	tertium *third*
	addidit *added*
	līberālissimī *very*
	generous

LVCIA ET QVINTVS
SVNT LIBERALISSIMI

About the language 1

1 In Stage 9, you met the dative case:

   mercātor **Metellae** togam trādidit.
   *The merchant handed over the toga **to Metella**.*

   Grumiō **hospitibus** cēnam parābat.
   *Grumio was preparing a meal **for the guests**.*

2 In Stage 11, you have met some further examples:

   Quīntus **Holcōniō** favet.   nōs **pistōrī** crēdimus.
   *Quintus gives support **to Holconius**.*   *We give our trust **to the baker**.*

3 The sentences above can be translated more simply:

   Quīntus Holcōniō favet.   nōs pistōrī crēdimus.
   Quintus supports Holconius.   *We trust the baker.*

4 Further examples:

   a nōs Āfrō favēmus.
   b vōs amīcīs crēditis.
   c mercātōrēs candidātō nostrō nōn crēdunt.

5 Notice the following use of the dative with the verb **placet**:

   placetne tibi?   mihi placet.
   Is it pleasing to you? *It is pleasing to me.*

   There are more natural ways of translating these examples, such as:

   Does it please you?   *Yes, it pleases me.*
   Do you like it?   *Yes, I do.*

6 Notice the dative of **nōs** and **vōs**:

   nōs sumus fortēs. deī **nōbīs** imperium dant.
   *We are brave. The gods give an empire **to us**.*

   vōs estis ignāvī. deī **vōbīs** nihil dant.
   *You are lazy. The gods give nothing **to you**.*

Lūcius Spurius Pompōniānus

in vīllā

Grumiō ē culīnā contendit. Clēmēns Grumiōnem videt.

Clēmēns:	babae! togam splendidam geris!	**babae!** *hey!*
Grumiō:	placetne tibi?	
Clēmēns:	mihi placet. quō festīnās, Grumiō?	**quō?** *where?*
Grumiō:	ad amphitheātrum contendō. Āfer fautōrēs exspectat.	5 **fautōrēs** *supporters*
Clēmēns:	num tū Āfrō favēs? Caecilius Holcōniō favet.	
Grumiō:	Āfer fautōribus quīnque dēnāriōs prōmīsit. Holcōnius fautōribus duōs dēnāriōs tantum prōmīsit. ego Āfrō faveō, quod vir līberālis est.	**quīnque** *five* **prōmīsit** *promised* 10 **tantum** *only*
Clēmēns:	sed tū servus es. cīvis Pompēiānus nōn es. Āfer cīvibus Pompēiānīs pecūniam prōmīsit.	
Grumiō:	Clēmēns, hodiē nōn sum Grumiō. hodiē sum Lūcius Spurius Pompōniānus!	
Clēmēns:	Lūcius Spurius Pompōniānus! mendācissimus coquus es!	15 **mendācissimus** *very deceitful*
Grumiō:	minimē! hodiē sum pistor Pompēiānus. hodiē nōs pistōrēs ad amphitheātrum convenīmus. nōs Āfrum ad forum dūcimus, ubi cīvēs ōrātiōnēs exspectant. ego ad amphitheātrum contendō. tū mēcum venīs?	**ad amphitheātrum** *at the amphitheater* **convenīmus** *gather, meet* 20 **ōrātiōnēs** *speeches*
Clēmēns:	tēcum veniō. Āfrō nōn faveō. dēnāriōs nōn cupiō, sed dē tē sollicitus sum. rem perīculōsam suscipis. *(exeunt.)*	**mēcum** *with me* **dē tē** *about you* **perīculōsam** *dangerous* **suscipis** *you are taking on* **exeunt** *they go out*

This notice reads: "Vote for Cnaeus Helvius Sabinus as aedile. He deserves public office."

prope amphitheātrum

multī pistōrēs ad amphitheātrum conveniunt. Grumiō et Clēmēns ad hanc turbam festīnant.

dīvīsor:	festīnāte! festīnāte! nōs Āfrum exspectāmus.	
Grumiō:	salvē, dīvīsor! ego sum Lūcius Spurius Pompōniānus	
	et hic *(Grumiō Clēmentem pulsat)* servus meus est.	5
	ego et Āfer amīcissimī sumus.	
dīvīsor:	ecce quīnque dēnāriī!	
	(dīvīsor Grumiōnī dēnāriōs dat. dīvīsor Grumiōnī	
	fūstem quoque trādit.)	
Grumiō:	Āfer mihi dēnāriōs, nōn fūstem prōmīsit.	10
Clēmēns:	Āfer vir līberālis est.	
Grumiō:	tacē, pessime serve!	
dīvīsor:	fūstēs ūtilissimī sunt. Holcōnius et amīcī sunt in forō.	
pistor:	ecce Āfer! Āfer adest!	
	(Āfer et fautōrēs per viās ad forum contendunt.)	15

dīvīsor *agent (hired to distribute bribes at elections)*
festīnāte! *hurry!*

tacē! *shut up! be quiet!*
ūtilissimī *very useful*

in forō

pistōrēs cum Clēmente et cum Grumiōne Āfrum ad forum dūcunt.

pistor prīmus:	Pompēiānī Āfrō favent.	
pistor secundus:	Āfer est melior quam Holcōnius.	
pistor tertius:	nōs Āfrō crēdimus.	
Clēmēns:	Grumiō! in forō sunt Holcōnius et amīcī.	5
	Holcōnium et amīcōs videō.	
Grumiō:	euge! fēminās videō, ancillās videō,	
	puellās … ēheu! Caecilium videō! Caecilius	
	cum Holcōniō stat! ad vīllam reveniō!	
Clēmēns:	Grumiō, manē!	10
	(Grumiō fugit.)	
mercātor prīmus:	Holcōnius est vir nōbilis.	
mercātor secundus:	Holcōnius melior est quam Āfer.	
mercātor tertius:	nōs mercātōrēs Holcōniō favēmus.	
	(pistōrēs et mercātōrēs conveniunt. īrātī sunt.)	15
pistor prīmus:	Holcōnius est asinus. vōs quoque estis	
	asinī, quod Holcōniō crēditis.	
mercātor prīmus:	Āfer est caudex. vōs quoque estis caudicēs,	
	quod Āfrō crēditis.	

Pompeians listening to a candidate speaking from the steps of the temple of Jupiter.

caudex *blockhead, idiot*

pistor secundus:	amīcī! mercātōrēs nōs "caudicēs" vocant.	20
	nōs nōn sumus caudicēs. fortissimī sumus.	
	fūstēs habēmus.	
mercātor secundus:	amīcī! pistōrēs nōs "asinōs" vocant. nōs nōn	
	sumus asinī. nōs fortiōrēs sumus quam	
	pistōrēs. magnōs fūstēs habēmus.	25
	(mercātōrēs et pistōrēs in forō pugnant.)	

*Candidates also made
speeches from a special
platform in the forum.*

in culīnā

Clēmēns in culīnā sedet. Grumiō intrat.

Clēmēns:	salvē, Pompōniāne! hercle! toga tua scissa est!		**scissa** *torn*
Grumiō:	ēheu! Holcōnius et amīcī in forō mē cēpērunt.		
	postquam fūstem meum cōnspexērunt, clāmābant,		
	"ecce pistor fortis!" tum mercātōrēs mē	5	
	verberāvērunt. dēnāriōs meōs rapuērunt. nunc		**rapuērunt** *seized,*
	nūllōs dēnāriōs habeō.		*grabbed*
Clēmēns:	ego decem dēnāriōs habeō!		
Grumiō:	decem dēnāriōs?		
Clēmēns:	Caecilius mihi decem dēnāriōs dedit, quod servus	10	
	fidēlis sum. postquam pistōrēs et mercātōrēs		
	pugnam commīsērunt, Caecilius mē cōnspexit. duo		
	pistōrēs Caecilium verberābant. dominus noster		
	auxilium postulābat. Caecilius mēcum ē forō effūgit.		**auxilium** *help*
	dominus noster mihi decem dēnāriōs dedit, quod	15	**effūgit** *escaped*
	līberālis est.		
Grumiō:	Caecilius est …		
Clēmēns:	valē, Pompōniāne!		
Grumiō:	quō festīnās, Clēmēns?		
Clēmēns:	ad portum festīnō. ibi Poppaea mē exspectat.	20	**ibi** *there*
	placetne tibi?		
Grumiō:	mihi nōn placet!		

About the language 2

1   So far you have met the following ways of asking questions in Latin:

- By tone of voice, indicated in writing by a question mark:

tū pecūniam dēbēs?	*Do you owe money?*
tū ānulum habēs?	*Do you have the ring?*

- By means of a question word such as **quis**, **quid**, **ubi**, **cūr**:

quis est Quīntus?	*Who is Quintus?*
quid tū facis?	*What are you doing?*
ubi est ānulus?	*Where is the ring?*
cūr tū lacrimās?	*Why are you crying?*

- By adding **-ne** to the first word of the sentence:

vōsne estis contentī?	*Are you satisfied?*
placetne tibi?	*Does it please you?*

- By means of the question word **num**. This word is used to suggest that the answer to the question will be "no." Notice the different ways of translating it:

num Quīntus timet?	*Surely Quintus is not afraid?*
	Quintus is not afraid, is he?
num tū Āfrō favēs?	*Surely you don't support Afer?*
	You don't support Afer, do you?

2   Further examples:

  a   cūr tū in hortō labōrās?
  b   quis est āthlēta ille?
  c   tū discum habēs?
  d   vōsne estis īrātī?
  e   ubi sunt mercātōrēs?
  f   quid quaeris, domina?
  g   tūne Pompēiānus es?
  h   quis vīnum portat?
  i   cēnam parās?
  j   num cēnam parās?

Practicing the language

1 Complete each sentence with the correct form of the verb from the box below. Then translate the sentence. Do not use any word more than once.

contendō	faveō
contendis	favēs
contendimus	favēmus
contenditis	favētis

a ego ad forum . . . . ego sum candidātus.
b tū Āfrō . . . . tū es stultus.
c ego Holcōniō . . . ., quod Holcōnius est candidātus optimus.
d nōs Holcōniō nōn . . . ., quod Holcōnius est asinus.
e Clēmēns, cūr tū ad portum . . . . ?
f vōs Āfrō . . . ., quod vōs estis pistōrēs.
g nōs ad vīllam . . . ., quod in forō sunt Holcōnius et amīcī.
h ēheu! cūr ē forō . . . .? vōs dēnāriōs meōs habētis!

2 Complete each sentence with the correct form of the noun. Then translate the sentence.

a Quīntus Sullae decem dēnāriōs dedit. Sulla . . . . in mūrō scrīpsit. (titulus, titulum)
b fūr thermās intrābat. . . . . eum agnōvit. (mercātor, mercātōrem)
c multī candidātī sunt in forō. ego . . . . videō. (Holcōnius, Holcōnium)
d ego ad portum currō. . . . . mē exspectat. (ancilla, ancillae)
e hodiē ad urbem contendō. in amphitheātrō sunt . . . . (leō, leōnēs)
f rhētor est īrātus. rhētor . . . . exspectat. (puerī, puerōs)
g fēminae sunt in tabernā. mercātōrēs fēminīs . . . . ostendunt. (stolae, stolās)
h postquam Holcōnius et amīcī Grumiōnem cēpērunt, quīnque . . . . rapuērunt. (dēnāriī, dēnāriōs)

Lūcia et Metella

Lūcia et māter sunt in hortō.

Metella:	Lūcia, pater tuus tibi marītum quaerit. itaque Holcōniō epistulam scrīpsit, quod Holcōnius multōs virōs cognōvit. hodiē Holcōnius respondit, "ego amīcum dīvitem et seniōrem habeō. amīcus est Umbricius. uxor est mortua et trēs līberōs habet. uxōrem novam quaerit." pater igitur tibi Umbricium ēlēgit. epistulam ad eum mīsit. placetne tibi?	
Lūcia:	ēheu! mihi nōn placet! *(lacrimat.)*	*10*
Metella:	quid dīcis? cūr lacrimās?	
Lūcia:	lacrimō, quod Alexandrum amō. iuvenis callidus est.	
Metella:	mea columba! Alexander est iuvenis callidus, sed Umbricius est vir nōbilis.	*15*
Lūcia:	sed Alexander mē dēlectat! *(Lūcia vehementer lacrimat et ex hortō currit.)*	

postrīdiē Metella Lūciam in ātrium vocat. Lūcia est trīstissima.

Metella:	pater tuus est īrātissimus. Umbricius epistulam mīsit.	*20*
Lūcia:	quid est in epistulā? cūr pater īrātus est?	
Metella:	Umbricius uxōrem novam iam habet! ancillam nūper līberāvit et eam in mātrimōnium dūxit. haec ancilla Umbricium et līberōs diū cūrāvit.	
Lūcia:	quam laeta sum! ego dīs grātiās maximās agō, quod mē servāvērunt.	*25*

Marginal glosses:

itaque *and so*
epistulam *letter*
cognōvit *knows*
dīvitem *rich*
seniōrem *older*

amō *love*

trīstissima *very sad*

iam *already*
nūper *recently*
eam in mātrimōnium dūxit *married her*
diū *for a long time*
dīs grātiās maximās agō *thank the gods very much*

Local government and elections

The Pompeians took local politics seriously, and the annual elections, which were held at the end of March, were very lively. As soon as the names of candidates were published, election fever gripped the town. Slogans appeared on the walls, groups of supporters held processions through the streets, and the candidates spoke at public meetings in the forum.

Every year, two pairs of officials were elected by the people. The senior pair, called **duovirī**, were responsible for hearing evidence and giving judgment in the law court. The other pair, called **aedīlēs**, had the task of supervising the public markets, the police force, the baths, places of public entertainment, the water supply, and sewers. It was their duty to see that the public services were efficiently run and the local taxes spent wisely.

In addition to these four officials, there was a town council of one hundred leading citizens, most of whom had already served as duoviri or aediles. New members were chosen not by the people but by the council itself.

The candidates wore a toga, specially whitened with chalk, in order to be easily recognized. The word **candidātus** is connected with **candidus** which means "dazzling white." As they walked around attended by their clients and greeting voters, their agents praised their qualities, made promises on their behalf, and distributed bribes in the form of money. This financial bribery was illegal but was widely practiced. Legal forms of persuasion included promises of games and entertainments if the candidate won. In fact, it was expected that those who were elected would show their gratitude to the voters by putting on splendid shows in the theater and amphitheater at their own expense.

A successful candidate would also be expected to contribute from his own wealth to the construction or repair of public buildings. The family of the Holconii, whose names often appear in the lists of Pompeian duoviri and aediles, were connected with the building of the large theater, and another wealthy family, the Flacci, helped to pay for other civic buildings. The Flacci also had a reputation for putting on first-class entertainments.

This tradition of public service was encouraged by the emperors and was an important part of Roman public life. It made it possible for a small town like Pompeii to enjoy benefits which could not have been paid for by local taxes alone. It also meant that men who wanted to take part in the government of their town had to be wealthy. They came from

The meeting place of the town council.

The public officials might provide free bread for the poor. One election slogan recommends a candidate who "brings good bread."

two groups: a small core of wealthy families, like the Holconii, whose members were regularly elected to the most important offices, and a larger, less powerful group which changed frequently.

Although public service was unpaid and was not a means of making money, it gave a man a position of importance in his town. The wide seats in the front row of the theater, which gave a close-up view of the chorus and actors, were reserved for him; he also had a special place close to the arena in the amphitheater. In due course the town council might erect a statue to him and he would have his name inscribed on any building to whose construction or repair he had contributed. The Romans were not modest people. They were eager for honor and fame among their fellow citizens. There was therefore no shortage of candidates to compete for these rewards at election time.

Caecilius does not seem to have stood as a candidate, although in many ways he was an outstanding citizen and had made a considerable fortune. Perhaps he preferred to concentrate on his business activities and was content to support candidates from the great political families like the Holconii.

Pompeii was free to run its own affairs. But if the local officials were unable to preserve law and order, the central government at Rome might take over and run the town. This actually happened after the famous riot in AD 59 described in Stage 8, when the people of nearby Nuceria quarreled with the Pompeians at a gladiatorial show given by Livineius Regulus, and many were killed or wounded. The Nucerians complained to the Emperor Nero; Regulus himself was sent into exile and games in Pompeii were banned for ten years.

We know that the temple of Fortuna Augusta, situated just to the north of the forum, was built largely by the generosity of Marcus Tullius who owned the whole of the site on which it was built.

Election notices

Many of the thousands of graffiti found in Pompeii refer to the elections held there in March, AD 79. Here are two of them:

Casellius for aedile.

We want Tiberius Claudius Verus for duovir.

Political supporters represented all kinds of people and interests. Sometimes they were groups of neighbors who lived in the same area as the candidate. They would certainly include the candidate's personal friends and his clients. Sometimes, however, appeals were made to particular trade groups. One notice reads:

Innkeepers, vote for Sallustius Capito!

Others are addressed to barbers, mule drivers, pack carriers, bakers, and fishermen. It is thought that most of the slogans

The town council might erect a statue to a leading politician. This is M. Holconius Rufus (also seen on page 147).

were organized by the agents of the candidates and groups of their supporters rather than by private individuals.

This method of electioneering by wall slogans naturally invited replies by rival supporters. One candidate, Vatia, was made to look ridiculous by this comment:

All the people who are fast asleep vote for Vatia.

Women could neither vote nor stand for public office. Nonetheless many, like Parthenope below, were very interested in local politics and expressed support for their favorite candidate:

Parthenope and Rufinus ask for Helvius Sabinus as aedile.

Other women supported the election of their family members. For example, Taedia Secunda supported her grandson's bid to become aedile:

Vote for Lucius Popidius Secundus as aedile. It's Taedia Secunda, his grandmother, who asks you to do so.

Women engaged in trade were particularly interested in the elections; graffiti survive in which female laundry workers, innkeepers, and bakers announce their political favorites. These election notices suggest that, when women decided which candidate to support, they were thinking of their own and their husbands' business interests, as well as the ties of family and friendship.

Painting election notices

It appears that these notices were often painted on the walls at night by lantern light. The streets were then more or less deserted, and so there was less risk of trouble from rival supporters. It was also easier at night to put up a ladder for an hour or two without causing congestion on the sidewalks.

At top right there is part of a notice advertising a fight of ten pairs of gladiators. It may have been paid for by a candidate in the elections.

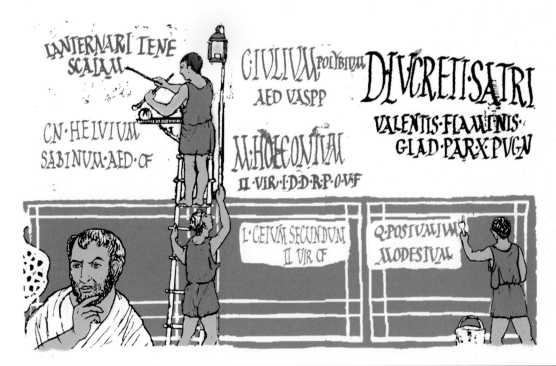

Vocabulary checklist 11

capit: cēpit	*takes*
cīvis	*citizen*
convenit: convēnit	*gathers, meets*
crēdit: crēdidit	*trusts, believes*
dē	*about*
favet: fāvit	*supports*
invītat: invītāvit	*invites*
it: iit	*goes*
legit: lēgit	*reads*
līberālis	*generous*
minimē!	*no!*
mūrus	*wall*
noster	*our*
nunc	*now*
placet: placuit	*it pleases*
prīmus	*first*
prōmittit: prōmīsit	*promises*
pugna	*fight*
senātor	*senator*
sollicitus	*worried, anxious*
stultus	*stupid*
valē!	*good-bye!*
verberat: verberāvit	*strikes, beats*
vir	*man*

L. Ceius Secundus is
proposed for aedile.

VESUVIUS

Stage 12

mōns īrātus

1   Syphāx et Fēlīx in portū stābant. amīcī
    montem spectābant.

2   Syphāx amīcō dīxit,
    "ego prope portum servōs vēndēbam.
    ego subitō sonōs audīvī."

3   Fēlīx Syphācī respondit,
    "tū sonōs audīvistī. ego tremōrēs sēnsī.
    ego prope montem ambulābam."

4 Poppaea et Lucriō in ātriō stābant.
   sollicitī erant.

5 Poppaea Lucriōnī dīxit,
      "ego in forō eram. ego tibi togam quaerēbam.
      ego nūbem mīrābilem cōnspexī."

6 Lucriō Poppaeae respondit,
      "tū nūbem cōnspexistī. sed ego cinerem
      sēnsī. ego flammās vīdī."

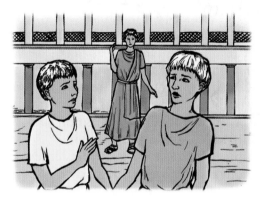

7 Thrasymachus et Diodōrus in forō
   erant. Alexander ad frātrēs contendit.

8 Alexander frātribus dīxit,
      "ego ad theātrum contendēbam. ego
      sonōs audīvī et tremōrēs sēnsī. vōs sonōs
      audīvistis? vōs tremōrēs sēnsistis?"

9 frātrēs Alexandrō respondērunt,
      "nōs tremōrēs sēnsimus et sonōs
      audīvimus. nōs nūbem mīrābilem
      vīdimus. nōs sollicitī sumus."

tremōrēs

tremōrēs *tremors*

When you have read this story, answer the questions opposite.

Caecilius cum Iūliō cēnābat. Iūlius in vīllā splendidā prope
Nūceriam habitābat.

    Iūlius Caeciliō dīxit, "ego sollicitus sum. ego in hortō herī
ambulābam et librum legēbam. subitō terra valdē tremuit. ego
tremōrēs sēnsī. quid tū agēbās?"   5

    "ego servō epistulās dictābam," inquit Caecilius. "ego quoque
tremōrēs sēnsī. postquam terra tremuit, Grumiō tablīnum
intrāvit et mē ad hortum dūxit. nōs nūbem mīrābilem vīdimus."

    "vōs timēbātis?" rogāvit Iūlius.

    "nōs nōn timēbāmus," Caecilius Iūliō respondit. "ego,   10
postquam nūbem cōnspexī, familiam meam ad larārium vocāvī.
tum nōs laribus sacrificium fēcimus."

    "hercle! vōs fortissimī erātis," clāmāvit Iūlius. "vōs tremōrēs
sēnsistis, vōs nūbem cōnspexistis. vōs tamen nōn erātis
perterritī."   15

    "nōs nōn timēbāmus, quod nōs laribus crēdēbāmus," inquit
Caecilius. "iamprīdem terra tremuit. iamprīdem tremōrēs vīllās
et mūrōs dēlēvērunt. sed larēs vīllam meam et familiam meam
servāvērunt. ego igitur sollicitus nōn sum."

    subitō servus triclīnium intrāvit.   20

    "domine, Clēmēns est in ātriō. Clēmēns ex urbe vēnit.
Caecilium quaerit," servus Iūliō dīxit.

    "nōn intellegō," Caecilius exclāmāvit. "ego Clēmentem ad
fundum meum māne mīsī."

    servus Clēmentem in triclīnium dūxit.   25

    "cūr tū ē fundō discessistī? cūr tū ad hanc vīllam vēnistī?"
rogāvit Caecilius.

    Clēmēns dominō et Iūliō rem tōtam nārrāvit.

tremuit *shook*
sēnsī *felt*
agēbās *were doing*
dictābam *was dictating*
nūbem *cloud*

larārium *shrine of the household gods*
laribus *household gods*
sacrificium *sacrifice*

iamprīdem *a long time ago*

fundum *farm*

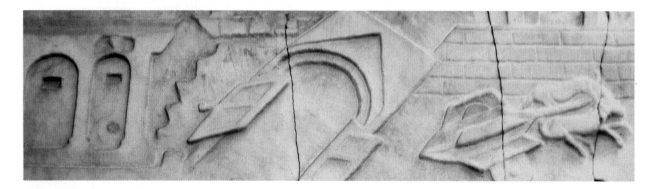

Questions

1 What was Caecilius doing at the beginning of this story? Where was he?

2 Why was Iulius worried?

3 What was Caecilius doing when the tremors began (line 6)?

4 What did Caecilius say that he and Grumio had seen when they went into the garden?

5 What two things did Caecilius say he had done next (lines 11–12)?

6 Why did Iulius think that Caecilius and his household were **fortissimī** (line 13)?

7 Why was Caecilius so sure that his Lares (gods) would look after his household (lines 17–19)?

8 **subitō servus triclīnium intrāvit** (line 20). What news did he bring?

9 What was Caecilius' reaction to the news? Why did he react in this way?

10 Read the last three lines of the story. Why do you think Clemens has come?

This is how Caecilius would have pictured a Lar, one of the gods who guarded his household.

Below and opposite: *At the time of the eruption, Caecilius' lararium was decorated with marble pictures of the earthquake that happened in AD 62 or 63.*

ad urbem

"ego ad fundum tuum contendī," Clēmēns dominō dīxit. "ego vīlicō epistulam tuam trādidī. postquam vīlicus epistulam lēgit, nōs fundum et servōs īnspiciēbāmus. subitō nōs ingentēs sonōs audīvimus. nōs tremōrēs quoque sēnsimus. tum ego montem spectāvī et nūbem mīrābilem vīdī."   5

"quid vōs fēcistis?" rogāvit Iūlius.

"nōs urbem petīvimus, quod valdē timēbāmus," respondit Clēmēns. "ego, postquam urbem intrāvī, clāmōrem ingentem audīvī. multī Pompēiānī per viās currēbant. fēminae cum īnfantibus per urbem festīnābant. fīliī et fīliae parentēs   10 quaerēbant. ego ad vīllam nostram pervēnī, ubi Quīntus mātrem et sorōrem in vīllā exspectābat. Metella et Lūcia aberant, quod in forō templum vīsitābant. Quīntus mē ad tē mīsit."

Caecilius statim Iūliō "valē" dīxit. ad urbem cum Clēmente festīnāvit, quod sollicitus erat. maxima turba viās complēbat, quod   15 Pompēiānī ē vīllīs festīnābant.

prope urbem Holcōnium cōnspexērunt. Holcōnius cum servīs ad portum fugiēbat.

"cūr vōs ad urbem contenditis? cūr nōn ad portum fugitis?" rogāvit Holcōnius.   20

"ad vīllam meam contendō," Caecilius Holcōniō respondit. "Metellam et līberōs quaerō. tū Metellam vīdistī? līberōs cōnspexistī?"

"ēheu!" clāmāvit Holcōnius. "ego vīllam splendidam habēbam. in vīllā erant statuae pulchrae et pictūrae pretiōsae.   25 iste mōns vīllam meam dēlēvit; omnēs statuae sunt frāctae."

"sed, amīce, tū uxōrem meam vīdistī?" rogāvit Caecilius.

"ego nihil dē Metellā scio. nihil cūrō," respondit Holcōnius.

"furcifer!" clāmāvit Caecilius. "tū vīllam tuam āmīsistī. ego uxōrem meam āmīsī!"   30

Caecilius, postquam Holcōnium vituperāvit, ad urbem contendit.

vīlicō *farm manager*
sonōs *noises*

parentēs *parents*
pervēnī *reached,*
          arrived at
templum *temple*

pretiōsae *precious*
iste mōns *that*
          (terrible) mountain
scio *know*
nihil cūrō *I don't care*

ad vīllam

postquam Caecilius urbem intrāvit, cinis iam dēnsior incidēbat. flammae ubīque erant. iter erat difficile, quod multī Pompēiānī viās complēbant.

Caecilius Clēmentī dīxit, "tū ad forum festīnā! Metellam et Lūciam quaere! ego ad vīllam nunc contendō, ubi Quīntus nōs exspectat." 5

dominus igitur ad vīllam contendit, servus ad forum festīnāvit. subitō Clēmēns magnum tremōrem sēnsit. mūrī ubīque dēcidērunt. Clēmēns ad proximum templum cucurrit, ubi erat tūtus. "dea Īsis mē servāvit," servus sibi dīxit. 10

Metella et Lūcia ē forō discessērunt et ad vīllam contendērunt. in urbe pavor maximus erat, quod fūmus dēnsissimus viās complēbat. Lūcia cum magnā difficultāte spīrābat.

Metella et fīlia tabernam dēsertam intrāvērunt et ad 15
terram dēcidērunt.

"ego maximē doleō, māter. dē vītā dēspērō," inquit Lūcia. "nōn facile spīrō."

"tē teneō, mea columba. sumus tūtae," inquit Metella.

"perterrita sum, māter," Lūcia susurrāvit. "ego tē amō." 20

"ego quoque tē amō, fīlia mea," respondit Metella. "ego semper tē amāvī."

cinis iam in viā dēnsissimē incidēbat. Lūcia et māter in tabernā dēsertā manēbant. Metella valdē perterrita erat. sonōs audīvit et tremōrēs sēnsit. nihil tamen dīxit. māter fīliam 25
aegram tenēbat et dē vītā suā nihil cūrābat. subitō tremor ingēns tabernam dēlēvit. Metella et fīlia in ruīnīs iacēbant.

cinis *ash*	
iam *now*	
dēnsior *thicker*	
incidēbat *was falling*	
flammae *flames*	
iter *journey, progress*	
difficile *difficult*	
proximum *nearest*	
tūtus *safe*	
dea *goddess*	
Īsis *Isis (Egyptian goddess)*	
pavor *panic*	
fūmus *smoke*	
cum magnā difficultāte *with great difficulty*	
spīrābat *was breathing*	
maximē *very greatly*	
dēnsissimē *very thickly*	
ruīnīs *ruins, wreckage*	

The goddess Isis, on a ring.

The temple of Isis, Pompeii.

fīnis

fīnis *end*

Clēmēns, postquam ē templō contendit, Metellam et Lūciam
per viās frūstrā quaerēbat. iam nūbēs ātra ad terram dēscendēbat;
iam cinis dēnsissimus incidēbat. plūrimī Pompēiānī iam dē urbe
suā dēspērābant. Clēmēns tamen nōn dēspērābat, sed obstinātē
vīllam petīvit, quod Caecilium quaerēbat. tandem ad vīllam   5
pervēnit. sollicitus ruīnās spectāvit. tōta vīlla ardēbat. Clēmēns
fūmum ubīque vīdit. per ruīnās tamen fortiter contendit et
dominum suum vocāvit. Caecilius tamen nōn respondit. subitō
canis lātrāvit. servus tablīnum intrāvit, ubi canis erat. Cerberus
dominum custōdiēbat.   10

    Caecilius in tablīnō moribundus iacēbat. mūrus sēmirutus
eum paene cēlābat. Clēmēns dominō vīnum dedit. Caecilius,
postquam vīnum bibit, sēnsim respīrāvit.

    "quid accidit, domine?" rogāvit Clēmēns.

    "ego ad vīllam vēnī," inquit Caecilius. "Metellam nōn vīdī!   15
Quīntum nōn vīdī! vīlla erat dēserta. tum ego ad tablīnum
contendēbam. subitō terra tremuit et pariēs in mē incidit.
vīdistīne Metellam et Lūciam?"

    "ēheu!" respondit Clēmēns. "ego eās diū quaesīvī, sed nōn
cōnspexī. ego igitur ad tē rediī."   20

    "tū es servus fidēlis et nōs omnēs cūrāvistī," inquit
Caecilius. "nunc abī! ego tē iubeō. dē vītā meā dēspērō. sine
dubiō Metella et līberī periērunt. nunc ego quoque sum
moritūrus."

    Clēmēns recūsāvit. in tablīnō obstinātē manēbat. Caecilius   25
iterum clāmāvit,

    "Clēmēns, abī! tē iubeō. fortasse Quīntus superfuit. quaere
Quīntum! hunc ānulum Quīntō dā!"

    Caecilius, postquam Clēmentī ānulum suum trādidit, statim
exspīrāvit. Clēmēns dominō trīste "valē" dīxit et ē vīllā discessit. 30

    Cerberus tamen in vīllā mānsit. dominum frūstrā
custōdiēbat.

ātra *black*
dēscendēbat *was coming down*
plūrimī *most*
obstinātē *stubbornly*

moribundus *almost dead*
sēmirutus *half-collapsed*
sēnsim *slowly, gradually*
respīrāvit *recovered breath, recovered consciousness*
accidit *happened*
pariēs *wall*
eās *them*

iubeō *order*
sine dubiō *without doubt*
periērunt *have died, have perished*
moritūrus *going to die*
recūsāvit *refused*
superfuit *has survived*

trīste *sadly*

City of the dead

Plaster casts have been made of the bodies of some of the people who died at Pompeii.

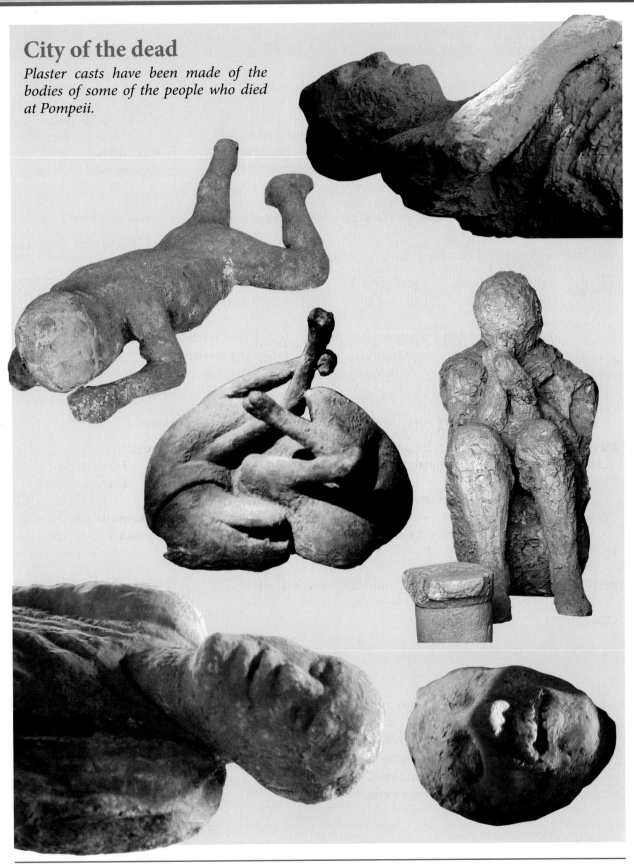

About the language

1 In Stage 6 you met the imperfect and perfect tenses:

IMPERFECT		PERFECT	
portābat	*s/he was carrying*	portāvit	*s/he carried*
portābant	*they were carrying*	portāvērunt	*they carried*

2 In Stage 12, you have met the imperfect and perfect tenses with "I," "you," and "we":

IMPERFECT			PERFECT		
(ego)	portābam	*I was carrying*	(ego)	portāvī	*I carried*
(tū)	portābās	*you (singular) were carrying*	(tū)	portāvistī	*you (singular) carried*
(nōs)	portābāmus	*we were carrying*	(nōs)	portāvimus	*we carried*
(vōs)	portābātis	*you (plural) were carrying*	(vōs)	portāvistis	*you (plural) carried*

ego, **tū**, **nōs**, and **vōs** are used only for emphasis and are usually left out.

3 The full imperfect and perfect tenses are:

IMPERFECT		PERFECT	
(ego)	portābam	(ego)	portāvī
(tū)	portābās	(tū)	portāvistī
	portābat		portāvit
(nōs)	portābāmus	(nōs)	portāvimus
(vōs)	portābātis	(vōs)	portāvistis
	portābant		portāvērunt

4 The words for "was" and "were" are as follows:

(ego)	eram	*I was*
(tū)	erās	*you (singular) were*
	erat	*s/he was*
(nōs)	erāmus	*we were*
(vōs)	erātis	*you (plural) were*
	erant	*they were*

5 Further examples:

   a portāvistis; portābātis; portābāmus
   b trāxī; trāxērunt; trāxistī
   c docēbant; docuī; docuimus
   d erātis; audīvī; trahēbam

The terrible mountain

Right: *A Pompeian painting of Vesuvius as Caecilius knew it, with vineyards on its fertile slopes.*

Below: *The mountain erupting in the eighteenth century; steam rising in the crater today; and the view from the sea, with the central cone replaced by two lower summits.*

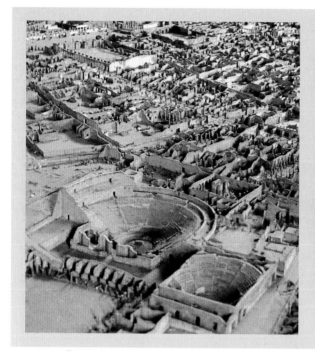

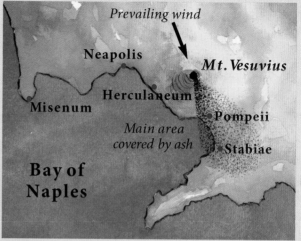

Above: *The area covered by ash from the eruption.*
Left: *Ash covered the city to the height of the walls shown in this model of the excavations. The theaters are in the foreground.*

The destruction and excavation of Pompeii

One night, in late summer or fall of AD 79, it rained hard; a strong wind blew and earth tremors were felt. During the following morning, Vesuvius, which had been an inactive volcano for many centuries, erupted with enormous violence, devastating much of the surrounding area. A huge mass of mud poured down the mountainside and swallowed the town of Herculaneum; hot stones and ash descended in vast quantities on Pompeii, burying everything to a depth of 15–20 feet (four-and-a-half to six meters). Most people, with vivid memories of the earthquake of seventeen years before, fled into the open countryside carrying a few possessions, but others remained behind, hoping that the storm would pass. They died, buried in the ruins of their homes or killed by the suffocating gas and intense heat of a pyroclastic flow (a fast-moving blast of hot gas and rock that accompanied the eruption).

The next day, the whole of Pompeii was a desert of white ash. Here and there the tops of buildings could be seen, and little groups of survivors struggled back to salvage what they could. They dug tunnels to get down to their homes and rescue money, furniture, and other valuables. But nothing could be done to excavate and rebuild the town itself. The site was abandoned; thousands of refugees made new homes in Naples and other Campanian towns. Gradually the ruins collapsed, a new layer of soil covered the site, and Pompeii disappeared from view.

A table is still in place in an upper room.

During the Middle Ages, nobody knew exactly where the town lay. Only a vague memory survived in the name "cività" by which the local people still called the low hill. But what city it was or whether there really was a city buried there, they neither knew nor cared.

The rediscovery of Pompeii and Herculaneum

The first remains of Pompeii were found in 1594, when an Italian architect called Fontana was constructing a water channel from the river Sarno to a nearby town. He discovered the remains of buildings and an inscription. But these were misunderstood as it was thought that a villa belonging to the famous Roman politician, Pompeius, had been discovered. Nothing much was done for another 150 years until, in 1748, Charles III, king of Naples, began to excavate the site in search of treasure. In 1763, the treasure seekers realized they were exploring the lost city of Pompeii. At Herculaneum the excavations were much more difficult because the volcanic mud had turned to hard rock and the town lay up to 40 feet (12 meters) below the new ground level. Tunneling down was slow and dangerous work.

In the early days of excavation, no effort was made to uncover the sites in an orderly way; the methods of modern archaeology were unknown. The excavators were not interested in uncovering towns in order to learn about the people who had lived there, but were looking for jewelry, statues, and other works of art, which were then taken away to decorate the palaces of kings and rich men.

Herculaneum. In the foreground are some of the excavated Roman buildings. The modern buildings in the distance lie above the unexcavated part of the town. The second floor of houses survives here.

Uncovering the temple of Isis in 1765.

At the beginning of the nineteenth century, however, the looting was stopped and systematic excavation began. Section by section, the soil and rubble were cleared. The most fragile and precious objects were taken to the National Museum in Naples, but everything else was kept where it was found. As buildings were uncovered, they were partly reconstructed with original materials to preserve them and make them safe for visitors.

From time to time, archaeologists found a hollow space in the solidified ash where an object of wood or other organic material perished. To find out what it was they poured liquid plaster into the hole, and when it hardened they carefully removed the surrounding ash, and were left with a perfect image of the original object. This work still continues, but now resin is used instead of plaster. In this way, many wooden doors and shutters have been discovered, and also bodies of human beings and animals.

A resin cast of a young woman's body. Unlike plaster, resin is transparent, and bones and jewelry can be seen through it. Resin is also less fragile than plaster.

Nowadays every bone and object discovered is carefully examined, recorded, and conserved. This skeleton was discovered at Herculaneum in 1982. The bones showed that she was a woman of about forty-five, with a protruding jaw; she had gum disease but no cavities in her teeth. Her wealth was clear from her rings, and the bracelets and earrings (below) that had been in her purse. By contrast, the bones of slaves may show signs of overwork and undernourishment.

The people died – the garden lives

Below: *Plaster casts are also made of tree roots, which helps identify the trees planted in the gardens and orchards of Pompeii. The position of each vine in this vineyard was identified and it has now been replanted.*

Right: *In the corner of the vineyard, just inside the walls, huddles a group of adults and children that failed to get away.*

At Herculaneum, where the town was hermetically sealed by the solidified mud, perishable objects have survived intact – for example, wooden doors and stairs, woven material, fishermen's nets, and wax tablets.

The work is not yet finished. Only about three-fifths of Pompeii have so far been uncovered and less of Herculaneum. Whenever a new house is opened up, the archaeologists find it just as it was abandoned. They may discover the remains of a meal, pots on the stove, coins in the tablinum, lampstands in various rooms, wall paintings (often only slightly damaged), the lead pipes which supplied water to the fountains in the garden, brooches, needles, jars of cosmetics, shoes, and toys; in fact all the hundreds of small things that went to make up a Roman home. If they are lucky, they may also discover the name of the family that lived there.

Thus, through the efforts of archaeologists, a remarkably detailed picture of the life of this ordinary Roman town has emerged from the disaster which destroyed it 2,000 years ago.

Vocabulary checklist 12

āmittit: āmīsit	*loses*
complet: complēvit	*fills*
custōdit: custōdīvit	*guards*
epistula	*letter*
flamma	*flame*
fortiter	*bravely*
frūstrā	*in vain*
fugit: fūgit	*runs away, flees*
fundus	*farm*
iacet: iacuit	*lies*
iam	*now*
igitur	*therefore*
mīrābilis	*strange, extraordinary*
mittit: mīsit	*sends*
mōns	*mountain*
optimē	*very well*
paene	*nearly, almost*
sentit: sēnsit	*feels*
tandem	*at last*
templum	*temple*
terra	*ground, land*
timet: timuit	*is afraid, fears*

You have also met these numbers:

ūnus	*one*
duo	*two*
trēs	*three*

*An abandoned lantern,
with the bones of its owner.*

LANGUAGE INFORMATION

Contents

Part One: About the language
Nouns

1   Words like **puella**, **servus**, **mercātor**, and **leō**, that indicate people, places, or things, are known as **nouns**. In Latin, nouns change their endings according to their function in a sentence (e.g. whether they are subjects or objects of a verb, etc.). These different forms of the same noun are called **cases**. Latin nouns belong to families called **declensions**. Each declension has its own set of endings for the various cases.

2   In Unit 1, you have met three cases and three declensions:

	first declension	*second declension*	*third declension*	
SINGULAR				
nominative	puella	servus	mercātor	leō
dative	puellae	servō	mercātōrī	leōnī
accusative	puellam	servum	mercātōrem	leōnem
PLURAL				
nominative	puellae	servī	mercātōrēs	leōnēs
dative	puellīs	servīs	mercātōribus	leōnibus
accusative	puellās	servōs	mercātōrēs	leōnēs

3   Review the way the cases are used:

The **nominative case** is used for the subject (whoever / whatever does the action of the verb):

    mercātor cantābat.   *The merchant was singing.*
    servī labōrābant.   *The slaves were working.*

The nominative case is also used for nouns which complete the verb **est**, since they refer back to the subject:

    Metella est **māter**.   *Metella is **the mother**.*
    Grumiō et Clēmēns sunt **servī**.   *Grumio and Clemens are **slaves**.*

The **dative case** indicates the indirect object of a verb, often translated into English by a phrase which begins with the preposition **to** or the preposition **for**, expressed or understood:

    senex **mercātōrī** pictūram ostendit.
    *The old man showed the painting **to the merchant**.*
    or
    *The old man showed **the merchant** the painting.*

    lībertī **puellīs** vīnum ferēbant.
    *The freedmen brought wine **for the girls**.*

Some Latin verbs are always completed by a noun in the dative case, even when the English equivalent does not seem to include **to** or **for**:

cīvēs **mercātōrī** crēdunt.	*The citizens trust **the merchant**.*
pistōrēs **Āfrō** favent.	*The bakers support **Afer**.*

The **accusative case** is used for the direct object (whoever / whatever receives the action of a verb):

Grumiō **puellam** salūtāvit.	*Grumio greeted **the girl**.*
Caecilius **servōs** vituperāvit.	*Caecilius cursed **the slaves**.*

4 In each pair of sentences below, the first sentence contains a noun in the nominative singular (in **boldface**). Translate that sentence. Then complete the second Latin sentence by writing the correct plural form of the noun in the nominative case. Translate the completed sentence.

For example:	**canis** in viā lātrāvit.		*The dog barked in the street.*
This becomes:	**canēs** in viā lātrāvērunt.		*The dogs barked in the street.*

a **servus** dominum timēbat.
..... dominum timēbant.

b **lībertus** in lectō recubuit.
..... in lectō recubuērunt.

c **poēta** versum recitābat.
..... versum recitābant.

d **hospes** vīllam intrāvit.
..... vīllam intrāvērunt.

e Sorex erat **āctor**.
Sorex et Actius erant ......

5 Translate each sentence, then change the word in **boldface** from the singular to the plural, and translate again.

For example:	puerī **servum** vīdērunt.		*The boys saw the slave.*
This becomes:	puerī **servōs** vīdērunt.		*The boys saw the slaves.*

a puerī **leōnem** vīdērunt.
b dominus **puellam** audīvit.
c centuriō **amīcum** salūtāvit.
d agricolae **gladiātōrem** laudāvērunt.

e cīvēs **servō** pecūniam trādidērunt.
f coquus **mercātōrī** cēnam parāvit.
g māter **fīliō** nōn crēdidit.
h ancillae **fēminae** respondērunt.

6 Translate each sentence, then change the word in **boldface** from the plural to the singular, and translate again.

For example: vēnālīciī **mercātōribus** pecūniam dedērunt.
The slave dealers gave money to the merchants.
This becomes: vēnālīciī **mercātōrī** pecūniam dedērunt.
The slave dealers gave money to the merchant.

a dominus **servōs** īnspexit.
b āthlētae **mercātōrēs** vituperāvērunt.
c vēnālīcius **ancillās** vēndēbat.
d senex **āctōrēs** spectābat.

e gladiātōrēs **leōnibus** cibum dedērunt.
f iuvenēs **puellīs** statuam ostendērunt.
g cīvēs **āctōribus** fāvērunt.
h puer **amīcīs** nōn respondit.

Verbs

1   Words like **portō**, **doceō**, **trahō**, **capiō**, and **audiō** are known as **verbs**. They usually indicate an action or a state of affairs.

2   In Latin the ending of the verb indicates the **person** who is doing the action. English uses pronoun subjects as follows:

	SINGULAR	PLURAL
first person	I	we
second person	you	you
third person	s/he, it	they

3   In Unit 1, you have met three tenses of verbs:

PRESENT TENSE	portō	*I carry*
	portās	*you (singular) carry*
	portat	*s/he carries*
	portāmus	*we carry*
	portātis	*you (plural) carry*
	portant	*they carry*
IMPERFECT TENSE	portābam	*I was carrying*
	portābās	*you (singular) were carrying*
	portābat	*s/he was carrying*
	portābāmus	*we were carrying*
	portābātis	*you (plural) were carrying*
	portābant	*they were carrying*
PERFECT TENSE	portāvī	*I carried*
	portāvistī	*you (singular) carried*
	portāvit	*s/he carried*
	portāvimus	*we carried*
	portāvistis	*you (plural) carried*
	portāvērunt	*they carried*

4   English has more than one way of translating each of these tenses.

- The present tense indicates an action or state happening now. **portō** can mean *I carry*, *I am carrying*, or *I do carry*.
- The imperfect tense indicates a repeated or incomplete past action or state. **portābam** can mean *I was carrying*, *I did carry*, *I used to carry*, or *I began to carry*.
- The perfect tense indicates a single or complete past action or state. **portāvī** can mean *I carried*, *I have carried*, or *I did carry*.

5 Just as nouns have declensions, verbs have families known as **conjugations**, based on the different vowel combinations found in front of the personal endings. The full table of verb endings met in Unit 1 is as follows:

	first conjugation	*second conjugation*	*third conjugation*	*fourth conjugation*
PRESENT TENSE	portō	doceō	trahō	audiō
	portās	docēs	trahis	audīs
	portat	docet	trahit	audit
	portāmus	docēmus	trahimus	audīmus
	portātis	docētis	trahitis	audītis
	portant	docent	trahunt	audiunt
IMPERFECT TENSE	portābam	docēbam	trahēbam	audiēbam
	portābās	docēbās	trahēbās	audiēbās
	portābat	docēbat	trahēbat	audiēbat
	portābāmus	docēbāmus	trahēbāmus	audiēbāmus
	portābātis	docēbātis	trahēbātis	audiēbātis
	portābant	docēbant	trahēbant	audiēbant
PERFECT TENSE	portāvī	docuī	trāxī	audīvī
	portāvistī	docuistī	trāxistī	audīvistī
	portāvit	docuit	trāxit	audīvit
	portāvimus	docuimus	trāximus	audīvimus
	portāvistis	docuistis	trāxistis	audīvistis
	portāvērunt	docuērunt	trāxērunt	audīvērunt

6 In paragraph 5 above, find the Latin words for:

a They were carrying; you (*singular*) were teaching; she was dragging; I was listening; you (*plural*) were carrying.

b He heard; they dragged; I taught; we listened; you (*singular*) carried.

c I teach; we drag; she hears; you (*plural*) drag; they carry.

7 Translate these examples of the present tense:

a ego dormiō; servus dormit; nōs dormīmus; servī dormiunt.

b servī labōrant; tū labōrās; servus labōrat; ego labōrō.

c intrant; intrās; intrat; intrō.

d sedēmus; sedeō; sedent; sedēs.

8 Further examples of all three tenses:

a servī ambulant; servī ambulābant; servī ambulāvērunt.

b servus labōrat; servus labōrābat; servus labōrāvit.

c clāmāmus; clāmābāmus; clāmāvimus.

d dormiunt; dormiēbant; dormīvērunt.

e parābās; parāvistī; parās.

f intrābam; intrāvī; intrō.

9 A few verbs which do not belong to any of the four conjugations are known as **irregular verbs**. This is the most important one:

PRESENT TENSE		IMPERFECT TENSE	
sum	*I am*	eram	*I was*
es	*you (singular) are*	erās	*you (singular) were*
est	*s/he, it is*	erat	*s/he, it was*
sumus	*we are*	erāmus	*we were*
estis	*you (plural) are*	erātis	*you (plural) were*
sunt	*they are*	erant	*they were*

10 Translate each of the following singular verb forms. Then convert each verb into its equivalent plural form and translate again.

> For example: portāvī   *I carried*
> This becomes: portāvimus   *we carried*

a trahis
b audīvistī
c veniēbam
d es
e scrīpsit
f fugiō
g circumspectābās
h mīsit
i tacuī
j erat

11 Translate each of the following plural verb forms. Then convert each verb into its equivalent singular form and translate again.

> For example: portāvimus   *we carried*
> This becomes: portāvī   *I carried*

a intrāmus
b timēbant
c cēpistis
d dormiunt
e sumus
f festīnābātis
g rīdēmus
h surrēxērunt
i celebrāvistis
j erāmus

Ways of forming the perfect tense

1 Most verbs in the first, second, and fourth conjugations form their perfect tenses in the following ways:

> First conjugation: like **portāvī**, e.g. **salūtāvī**
> Second conjugation: like **docuī**, e.g. **terruī**, **appāruī**
> Fourth conjugation: like **audīvī**, e.g. **dormīvī**, **custōdīvī**.

2 But there are many other ways in which verbs, especially in the third conjugation, may form their perfect tense. Note the following patterns:

a A consonant change, most often to an **s** or an **x**:

PRESENT		PERFECT	
discēdit	*s/he leaves*	disce**ss**it	*s/he left*
mittit	*s/he sends*	mī**s**it	*s/he sent*
trahit	*s/he drags*	trā**x**it	*s/he dragged*
dīcit	*s/he says*	dī**x**it	*s/he said*

(Some English verbs follow the same pattern, e.g. "send – sent," "make – made.")

b A vowel change:

PRESENT		PERFECT	
facit	*s/he makes*	f**ē**cit	*s/he made*
capit	*s/he takes*	c**ē**pit	*s/he took*

(Some English verbs follow the same pattern, e.g. "take – took," "run – ran.")

c Adding an extra syllable:

PRESENT		PERFECT	
currit	*s/he runs*	**cu**currit	*s/he ran*
dat	*s/he gives*	**de**dit	*s/he gave*

(Many English verbs add an extra syllable "-ed" at the end, e.g. "add – added," "point – pointed." The Latin verbs add their extra syllable on the front.)

d Changing the pronunciation (usually by making a short vowel long):

PRESENT		PERFECT	
venit	*s/he comes*	v**ē**nit	*s/he came*
fugit	*s/he flees*	f**ū**git	*s/he fled*

(Some English verbs follow the same pattern, e.g. "read – read.")

e No change:

PRESENT		PERFECT	
ostendit	*s/he shows*	ostendit	*s/he showed*
contendit	*s/he hurries*	contendit	*s/he hurried*

(Some English verbs follow the same pattern, e.g. "hit – hit," "put – put.")

Unfortunately, as with English, there are many patterns and many exceptions. Learning the forms as they appear on Vocabulary checklists and by practice in reading stories and writing exercises is still the best way to master recognition.

3 Translate each of the following present tense verb forms. Then convert each verb into its equivalent perfect tense form and translate again.

> For example: portāmus   *we carry*
> This becomes: portāvimus   *we carried*

a laudat
b venīmus
c quaeritis
d faciunt
e dūcō
f tacēs
g prōcēdimus
h dormit
i reddō
j petitis

4 Translate each of the following perfect tense verb forms. Then convert each verb into its equivalent present tense form and translate again.

> For example: portāvimus   *we carried*
> This becomes: portāmus   *we carry*

a rogāvī
b dedimus
c īnspexit
d ostendit
e cucurristis
f respondimus
g audīvistī
h timuī
i laudāvērunt
j clāmāvistis

Word order

1 The following word order is very common in Latin:

    Milō discum īnspexit.   *Milo looked at the discus.*
    mercātor togam vēndidit.   *The merchant sold the toga.*

2 From Stage 7 on, you have learned a slightly different example of the above word order:

    discum īnspexit.   *He looked at the discus.*
    togam vēndidit.   *He sold the toga.*
    amīcum salūtāvit.   *She greeted the friend.*
    theātrum intrāvērunt.   *They entered the theater.*

3 The following sentences are similar to those in paragraphs 1 and 2:

  a spectātōrēs Milōnem laudāvērunt.
  b Milōnem laudāvērunt.
  c senex agricolam cōnspexit.
  d agricolam cōnspexit.
  e canēs et servī leōnem necāvērunt.
  f mercātor poētam et vēnālīcium vīdit.
  g poētam vīdit.
  h āthlētam salūtāvit.
  i mē salūtāvit.
  j tē salūtāvērunt.
  k Metella clāmōrem audīvit.
  l clāmōrem audīvit.

4 Further examples:

  a Caecilius amīcum salūtat; amīcum salūtat.
  b ego amīcōs salūtāvī; amīcōs salūtāvī.
  c nōs gladiātōrēs spectābāmus; clāmōrem audīvimus.
  d vōs cibum cōnsūmēbātis; vīnum bibēbātis; Grumiōnem laudāvistis.

5 From Stage 9 on, you have met longer sentences, involving the dative. The following word order is common in Latin:

    vēnālīcius mercātōrī ancillam ostendit.
    The slave dealer showed the slave girl to the merchant.

6 Further examples:

  a iuvenis Milōnī discum trādidit.
  b Metella fīliō dōnum ēmit.
  c dominus ancillīs signum dedit.
  d nūntiī cīvibus spectāculum nūntiāvērunt.
  e Quīntus mercātōrī et amīcīs togam ostendit.

Longer sentences with *postquam* and *quod*

1   Compare these two sentences:

    Pompēiānī gladiātōrēs vīdērunt.
    The Pompeians saw the gladiators.

    Pompēiānī, postquam amphitheātrum intrāvērunt, gladiātōrēs vīdērunt.
    The Pompeians, after they entered the amphitheater, saw the gladiators.

    Or, in more natural English:
    After the Pompeians entered the amphitheater, they saw the gladiators.

2   The next example is similar:

    servī umbram timēbant.
    The slaves were afraid of the ghost.

    servī, quod erant ignāvī, umbram timēbant.
    The slaves, because they were cowardly, were afraid of the ghost.
    Or:
    Because the slaves were cowardly, they were afraid of the ghost.

3   **postquam** and **quod** are **conjunctions** introducing subordinate clauses. A **subordinate clause** is one that cannot stand by itself but is dependent on (i.e. subordinate to) the rest of the sentence, which is called the **main clause**.

4   Further examples:

a   Metella ad tablīnum festīnāvit.
    Metella, postquam ē culīnā discessit, ad tablīnum festīnāvit.

b   amīcī Fēlīcem laudāvērunt.
    amīcī, postquam fābulam audīvērunt, Fēlīcem laudāvērunt.

c   tuba sonuit.
    postquam Rēgulus signum dedit, tuba sonuit.

d   Caecilius nōn erat sollicitus.
    Caecilius nōn erat sollicitus, quod in cubiculō dormiēbat.

e   Nūcerīnī fūgērunt.
    Nūcerīnī, quod Pompēiānī erant īrātī, fūgērunt.

Part Two: Vocabulary

1 Nouns and adjectives are usually listed in their nominative singular form, as follows:

> **servus**   *slave*
> **magnus**   *big, large, great*
> **ancilla**   *slave girl, slave woman*
> **auxilium**   *help*

2 Third declension nouns, however, are listed with both nominative and accusative singular forms, as follows:

> **leō: leōnem**   *lion*

This kind of entry means that **leō** is the nominative singular form and **leōnem** the accusative singular form of the Latin word for "lion."

3 *Practice examples*

Find the nominative singular of the following words:

> novāculam
> lupum
> sanguinem
> stēllae
> īnfantēs
> mūrō
> cīvibus

4 Verbs are usually listed in the third person singular form of their present and perfect tenses, as follows:

> **parat: parāvit**   *prepares*

This kind of entry indicates that **parat** means *s/he, it prepares* and **parāvit** means *s/he, it prepared* or *has prepared*.

5 If only one of these two tenses is used in Unit 1, then only that tense is listed. For example:

> **exspīrāvit**   *died*

6 Sometimes, if the perfect tense looks somewhat different from the present tense, it will be listed separately, as well as with its present tense. For example:

> **cēpit, fēcit**

7 *Practice examples*

Find the meaning of the following words, some of which are in the present tense and some in the perfect:

laudat
laudāvit
respondit
respondet
intellēxit
accēpit
salūtāvit
tenet
dēposuit
fūgit

8 Phrases (e.g. **cōnsilium capit**, **rem intellegit**, etc.) are listed under both words of the phrase.

9 Some Latin words have more than one possible translation. Always choose the most suitable translation for the sentence you are working on.

cīvēs perterritī urbem petēbant.
The terrified citizens were heading for the city.

iuvenēs īrātī mercātōrem petīvērunt.
The angry young men attacked the merchant.

10 Where a word appears in a Vocabulary checklist in Stages 1-12, it is marked with the relevant Stage number in the following pages. For example:

1 **canis: canem** *dog*

This means that **canis** appears as a Vocabulary checklist word in Stage 1.

a

6	aberat	*was absent*
6	abest	*is gone, is absent*
10	abit: abiit	*goes away*
	accidit	*happened*
10	accipit: accēpit	*accepts*
	accūsat	*accuses*
	āctor: āctōrem	*actor*
3	ad	*to, at*
	addidit	*added*
5	adest	*is here*
	adiuvat	*helps*
	administrat	*looks after*
5	adsunt	*are here*
	aedificat	*builds*
	aeger: aegrum	*sick, ill*
	Aegyptius	*Egyptian*
4	agit	*does, acts*
	fābulam agit	*acts in a play*
	grātiās agit	*thanks, gives thanks*
	negōtium agit	*does business, works*
8	agitat: agitāvit	*chases, hunts*
9	agnōscit: agnōvit	*recognizes*
5	agricola	*farmer*
	alius	*other, another*
	alter: alterum	*the other, the second*
	amat: amāvit	*loves*
5	ambulat: ambulāvit	*walks*
	amīcissimus	*very friendly*
2	amīcus	*friend*
12	āmīsit	*lost*
	amphitheātrum	*amphitheater*
2	ancilla	*slave girl, slave woman*
	animal	*animal*
	antīquus	*old, ancient*
4	ānulus	*ring*
	anxius	*anxious*
	aper: aprum	*boar*
	aperit: aperuit	*opens*
	apodytērium	*changing room*
	appāret: appāruit	*appears*
	architectus	*builder, architect*

	ardet	*burns, is on fire*
	arēna	*arena*
	argentāria	*banker's stall*
	argentārius	*banker*
	argūmentum	*proof, evidence*
	artifex: artificem	*artist, craftsperson*
	asinus	*ass, donkey*
	āter: ātrum	*black*
	āthlēta	*athlete*
	ātrium	*atrium, main room*
	attonitus	*astonished*
	auctor: auctōrem	*creator*
	audācissimē	*very boldly*
5	audit: audīvit	*hears, listens to*
	aurae	*air*
	auxilium	*help*
	avārus	*miser*

b

	babae!	*hey!*
	barba	*beard*
	barbarus	*barbarian*
	basilica	*court building, law court*
	benignus	*kind*
	bēstia	*wild animal, beast*
	bēstiārius	*a gladiator who fights animals, beast fighter*
3	bibit: bibit	*drinks*

c

	caelum	*sky*
10	callidus	*clever, cunning*
	callidior	*cleverer, more cunning*
	candidātus	*candidate*
1	canis: canem	*dog*
	cantat: cantāvit	*sings*
11	capit: cēpit	*takes*
	cōnsilium capit	*makes a plan, has an idea*
	caudex: caudicem	*blockhead, idiot*
	caupō: caupōnem	*innkeeper*
	cautē	*cautiously*
	cēlat	*hides*

	celebrat	celebrates		11	convenit	gathers, meets
9	celeriter	quickly			convincit	convicts, finds guilty
	quam celerrimē	as quickly as possible		4	coquit: coxit	cooks
2	cēna	dinner		1	coquus	cook
7	cēnat: cēnāvit	eats dinner, dines			cotīdiē	every day
	centuriō:				coxit	cooked
	centuriōnem	centurion		11	crēdit	trusts, believes, has
	cēpit	took, has taken				faith in
	cēra	wax, wax tablet			crīnēs: crīnēs	hair
	cervus	deer		6	cubiculum	bedroom
	Christiānus	Christian			cucurrit	ran
2	cibus	food			culīna	kitchen
	cinis: cinerem	ash		7	cum	with
3	circumspectat:			9	cupit	wants
	circumspectāvit	looks around		4	cūr?	why?
11	cīvis: cīvem	citizen			cūrat: cūrāvit	takes care of
3	clāmat: clāmāvit	shouts			nihil cūrō	I don't care
5	clāmor: clāmōrem	shout, uproar		5	currit: cucurrit	runs
	clausit	shut, closed		12	custōdit	guards
	clausus	closed				
	cōgitat	considers			**d**	
	rem cōgitat	considers the problem		9	dat: dedit	gives
	cognōvit	knows			fābulam dat	puts on a play
	columba	dove		11	dē	down from; about
	commīsit	began			dea	goddess
	commōtus	moved, affected			dēbet	owes
12	complet	fills			decem	ten
	compōnit	arranges			dēcidit	fell down
	comprehendit	arrested			dēcipit	deceives, tricks
	cōnfēcit	finished			dedit	gave, has given
	rem cōnfēcit	finished the job			dēiēcit	threw down
	coniēcit	hurled, threw			deinde	then
	cōnsentit	agrees			dēlectat: dēlectāvit	delights, pleases
	cōnsilium	plan, idea			dēlēvit	destroyed
	cōnsilium capit	makes a plan, has an idea			dēliciae	darling
					dēnārius	a denarius (a small coin)
7	cōnspexit	caught sight of			dēnsissimē	very thickly
8	cōnsūmit: cōnsūmpsit	eats			dēnsus	thick
5	contendit: contendit	hurries			dēpōnit: dēposuit	puts down, takes off
	contentiō:				dēscendit	comes down
	contentiōnem	argument			dēsertus	deserted
10	contentus	satisfied			dēsistit	stops
	contrōversia	debate			dēspērat	despairs

	dēstrīnxit	*drew, pulled out*
	deus	*god*
	dīcit: dīxit	*says*
	dictat	*dictates*
9	diēs: diem	*day*
	diēs nātālis:	
	diem nātālem	*birthday*
	difficilis	*difficult*
	difficultās	*difficulty*
	dīligenter	*carefully*
	discēdit: discessit	*departs, leaves*
	discit	*learns*
	discus	*discus*
	dissentit	*disagrees, argues*
	diū	*for a long time*
	dīves: dīvitem	*rich*
	dīvīsor: dīvīsōrem	*distributor, a man hired to bribe voters*
	dīxit	*said*
	docet: docuit	*teaches*
	doctus	*educated, skillful*
	dolet	*hurts, is in pain*
	domina	*lady (of the house)*
2	dominus	*master (of the house)*
	dōnum	*present, gift*
2	dormit: dormīvit	*sleeps*
	dubium	*doubt*
8	dūcit: dūxit	*leads, takes*
	in mātrimōnium dūxit	*married*
12	duo	*two*

e

4	ē	*out of, from*
	eam	*her, it*
	eās	*them*
	ēbrius	*drunk*
3	ecce!	*look!*
	ēdit: ēdidit	*presents*
	effūgit	*escaped*
4	ego	*I*
4	ēheu!	*oh dear! oh no!*
	ēlēgit	*chose*

6	emit: ēmit	*buys*
9	ēmīsit	*threw, sent out*
	eōs	*them*
12	epistula	*letter*
	ērādit: ērāsit	*erases*
	erat	*was*
	ērubēscit	*blushes*
	es	*you (singular) are*
1	est	*is*
	estis	*you (plural) are*
	ēsurit	*is hungry*
3	et	*and*
	euge!	*hurray!*
8	eum	*him, it*
	ēvānuit	*vanished*
	ēvītāvit	*avoided*
	ēvolāvit	*flew*
	ex	*out of, from*
	excitāvit	*woke up*
10	exclāmāvit	*exclaimed, shouted*
3	exit	*goes out*
	expedītus	*lightly armed*
	explicāvit	*explained*
3	exspectat	*waits for*
	exspīrāvit	*died*
	extrāxit	*pulled out*

f

5	fābula	*play, story*
	fābulam agit	*acts in a play*
	fābulam dat	*puts on a play*
8	facile	*easily*
7	facit: fēcit	*makes, does*
	familia	*household*
	fautor: fautōrem	*supporter*
11	favet	*favors, supports*
	fēcit	*made, did*
	fēlēs: fēlem	*cat*
	fēlīx: fēlīcem	*lucky*
5	fēmina	*woman*
6	ferōciter	*fiercely*
8	ferōx: ferōcem	*fierce, ferocious*
	ferōcissimus	*very fierce*

9	fert	brings, carries
6	festīnat: festīnāvit	hurries
	fidēlis	faithful, loyal
1	fīlia	daughter
1	fīlius	son
	fīnis: fīnem	end
12	flamma	flame
	fluit	flows
	fortasse	perhaps
6	fortis	brave
	fortissimus	very brave
12	fortiter	bravely
	forum	forum, business center
	frāctus	broken
10	frāter: frātrem	brother
	fremit: fremuit	roars
12	frūstrā	in vain
12	fugit: fūgit	runs away, flees
	fūmus	smoke
	fūnambulus	tightrope walker
12	fundus	farm
6	fūr: fūrem	thief
	furcifer!	scoundrel! crook!
	fūstis: fūstem	club, stick

g

	gēns: gentem	family
	gerit	wears
	gladiātor: gladiātōrem	gladiator
8	gladius	sword
	Graecia	Greece
	Graeculus	poor Greek
	Graecus	Greek
	grātiae	thanks
	grātiās agit	thanks, gives thanks
	graviter	seriously
	gustat: gustāvit	tastes

h

4	habet	has
10	habitat	lives
	hae	these
	haec	this

	hanc	this
	hausit	drained, drank up
	hercle!	by Hercules! good heavens!
7	heri	yesterday
8	hic	this
	hoc	this
5	hodiē	today
9	homō: hominem	person, man
1	hortus	garden
9	hospes: hospitem	guest
	hūc	here, to this place
	hunc	this

i

12	iacet	lies, rests
12	iam	now, already
	iamprīdem	a long time ago
3	iānua	door
	ībat	was going
	ibi	there
12	igitur	therefore, and so
8	ignāvus	cowardly, lazy
	illam	that
9	ille	that
	imitātor: imitātōrem	imitator
	immōtus	still, motionless
10	imperium	empire
	impetus	attack
	imprimit	presses
	impūne	safely
1	in	in, on; into, onto
	incendium	fire, blaze
	incidit: incidit	falls
	incitat	urges on, encourages
	induit	put on
	īnfāns: īnfantem	baby, child
	īnfēlīx: īnfēlīcem	unlucky
7	ingēns: ingentem	huge
	inimīcus	enemy
4	inquit	says, said
	īnsānus	insane, crazy
	īnscrīptiō:	
	īnscrīptiōnem	inscription, notice, writing

9	īnspicit: īnspexit	looks at, inspects, examines
	īnstitor: īnstitōrem	street vendor
7	intellegit: intellēxit	understands
	rem intellegit	understands the truth
6	intentē	closely, carefully
	interfēcit	killed
2	intrat: intrāvit	enters
	intrō īte!	go inside!
	intus	inside
10	invēnit	found
11	invītat: invītāvit	invites
3	īrātus	angry
	iste	that
11	it	goes
	ita	in this way
	ita vērō	yes
	itaque	and so
	iter	journey, progress
9	iterum	again
	iubet	orders
4	iūdex: iūdicem	judge
5	iuvenis: iuvenem	young man, young woman

l

1	labōrat	works
7	lacrimat	cries, weeps
	laetē	happily
2	laetus	happy
	lambit	licks
	lapideus	made of stone
	larārium	shrine of the household gods
	larēs	household gods
	latet	lies hidden
	Latīnus	Latin
	lātrat: lātrāvit	barks
2	laudat: laudāvit	praises
	lectus	couch
11	legit: lēgit	reads
3	leō: leōnem	lion
10	liber: librum	book
11	līberālis	generous
	līberāvit	freed, set free
	līberī	children

6	lībertus	freedman, ex-slave
	lingua	tongue, language
	locus	place
	longē	far, a long way
	longus	long
	lūcet	shines
	lūna	moon
	lupus	wolf

m

	magnificē	splendidly, magnificently
	magnificus	splendid, magnificent
3	magnus	big, large, great
	maior	bigger, larger, greater
	māne	in the morning
9	manet: mānsit	remains, stays
	marītus	husband
1	māter: mātrem	mother
	mātrimōnium	marriage
	in mātrimōnium dūxit	married
	maximē	very greatly
	maximus	very big, very large, very great
	mē	me
	mēcum	with me
9	medius	middle
	melior	better
	mendācissimus	very deceitful
4	mendāx: mendācem	liar
	mēnsa	table
2	mercātor: mercātōrem	merchant
5	meus	my, mine
	mihi	to me
11	minimē!	no!
12	mīrābilis	extraordinary, strange
	miserandus	pitiful, pathetic
	missiō: missiōnem	release
12	mittit: mīsit	sends
12	mōns: montem	mountain
	morbus	illness
	moribundus	almost dead, dying
	moritūrus	going to die

	mors: mortem	*death*
	mortiferus	*deadly*
7	mortuus	*dead*
9	mox	*soon*
5	multus	*much*
5	multī	*many*
	murmillō:	
	murmillōnem	*murmillo, a kind of heavily armed gladiator*
11	mūrus	*wall*

n

7	nārrāvit	*told, narrated*
	rem nārrāvit	*told the story*
	nāsus	*nose*
	nauta	*sailor*
3	nāvis: nāvem	*ship*
7	necāvit	*killed*
	negōtium	*business*
	negōtium agit	*does business, works*
	nēmō: nēminem	*no one, nobody*
7	nihil	*nothing*
	nihil cūrō	*I don't care*
	nimium	*too much*
	nisi	*except*
	nōbilis	*noble, of noble birth*
	nōbīs	*to us*
3	nōn	*not*
10	nōs	*we, us*
11	noster: nostrum	*our*
	nōtus	*well-known, famous*
	nōtissimus	*very well-known*
	novācula	*razor*
	novus	*new*
	nox: noctem	*night*
	nūbēs: nūbem	*cloud*
	Nūcerīnī	*people of Nuceria*
	nūllus	*no*
	num?	*surely ... not?*
	numerat	*counts*
	numquam	*never*
11	nunc	*now*
10	nūntiat: nūntiāvit	*announces*
8	nūntius	*messenger*

	nūper	*recently*

o

	obdormīvit	*went to sleep*
	obstinātē	*stubbornly*
	occupātus	*busy*
9	offert	*offers*
	olfēcit	*smelled, sniffed*
6	ōlim	*once, some time ago*
7	omnis	*all*
12	optimē	*very well*
5	optimus	*very good, excellent, best*
	ōrātiō: ōrātiōnem	*speech*
9	ostendit: ostendit	*shows*
	ōtiōsus	*on holiday, idle, taking time off*

p

12	paene	*nearly, almost*
	palaestra	*palaestra, exercise area*
	pānis: pānem	*bread*
7	parat: parāvit	*prepares*
	parātus	*ready*
	parce!	*spare me! have pity on me!*
	parēns: parentem	*parent*
	pariēs: parietem	*wall*
6	parvus	*small, little*
	pāstor: pāstōrem	*shepherd*
1	pater: patrem	*father*
	pauper: pauperem	*poor*
	pauperrimus	*very poor*
	pāvō: pāvōnem	*peacock*
	pavor: pavōrem	*panic*
10	pāx: pācem	*peace*
4	pecūnia	*money*
6	per	*through*
	percussit	*struck*
	perīculōsus	*dangerous*
	perīculum	*danger*
	periit	*died, perished*
4	perterritus	*terrified*
	pervēnit	*reached, arrived at*
8	pēs: pedem	*foot, paw*
	pessimus	*worst, very bad*

	pestis: pestem	*pest, rascal*
5	petit: petīvit	*heads for, attacks, seeks*
	philosophus	*philosopher*
	pictor: pictōrem	*painter, artist*
	pictūra	*painting, picture*
	pingit	*paints*
	piscīna	*fishpond*
	pistor: pistōrem	*baker*
11	placet	*it pleases, suits*
5	plaudit: plausit	*applauds, claps*
	plēnus	*full*
	plūrimus	*most*
	pōculum	*cup (often for wine)*
4	poēta	*poet*
	pollex: pollicem	*thumb*
	Pompēiānus	*Pompeian*
	pōns: pontem	*bridge*
8	porta	*gate*
3	portat: portāvit	*carries*
	porticus	*colonnade*
10	portus	*harbor*
9	post	*after*
	posteā	*afterwards*
6	postquam	*after, when*
	postrēmō	*finally, lastly*
	postrīdiē	*(on) the next day*
8	postulat: postulāvit	*demands*
	posuit	*placed, put up*
	praemium	*profit, reward*
	pretiōsus	*expensive, precious*
11	prīmus	*first*
	probat	*proves*
	rem probat	* proves the case*
	probus	*honest*
9	prōcēdit: prōcessit	*advances, proceeds*
11	prōmīsit	*promised*
7	prope	*near*
	proprius	*right, proper*
	prōvocāvit	*called out, challenged*
	proximus	*nearest*
5	puella	*girl*
8	puer: puerum	*boy*
11	pugna	*fight*
8	pugnat: pugnāvit	*fights*

9	pulcher: pulchrum	*beautiful, handsome*
	pulcherrimus	* very beautiful,*
		* very handsome*
6	pulsat: pulsāvit	*hits, knocks at, punches*
	pȳramis: pȳramidem	*pyramid*

q

	quadrāgintā	*forty*
4	quaerit: quaesīvit	*searches for, looks for*
10	quam	*than, how*
	quam celerrimē	* as quickly as possible*
	quantī?	*how much?*
	quid?	*what?*
	quiētus	*quiet*
	quīndecim	*fifteen*
	quīnquāgintā	*fifty*
	quīnque	*five*
4	quis?	*who?*
	quō?	*where, where to?*
6	quod	*because*
2	quoque	*also, too*

r

	rapuit	*seized, grabbed*
	recitat: recitāvit	*recites*
	recumbit: recubuit	*lies down, reclines*
	recūsāvit	*refused*
4	reddit	*gives back*
	rediit	*went back, came back,*
		* returned*
6	rēs: rem	*thing*
	rem cōgitat	* considers the problem*
	rem cōnfēcit	* finished the job*
	rem intellegit	* understands the truth*
	rem nārrāvit	* told the story*
	rem probat	* proves the case*
	respīrāvit	*recovered breath, recovered*
		* consciousness*
3	respondet: respondit	*replies*
	rētiārius	*retiarius, gladiator who*
		* fought with a net*
	retinet	*holds back, keeps*
9	revenit	*comes back, returns*
	rhētor: rhētorem	*teacher*

3	rīdet: rīsit	laughs, smiles
	rīdiculus	ridiculous, silly
7	rogāvit	asked
	Rōma	Rome
	Rōmānus	Roman
	ruīna	ruin, wreckage
	ruit: ruit	rushes

s

	sacrificium	offering, sacrifice
8	saepe	often
	salit	leaps, jumps
	salūs: salūtem	safety
2	salūtat: salūtāvit	greets
3	salvē!	hello!
8	sanguis: sanguinem	blood
4	satis	enough
	scaena	stage, scene
	scissus	torn
	scit	knows
6	scrībit: scrīpsit	writes
	scrīptor: scrīptōrem	signwriter
	sculptor: sculptōrem	sculptor
	scurrīlis	rude
	secat	cuts
	secundus	second
4	sed	but
1	sedet	sits
	sella	chair
	sēmirutus	half-collapsed
	sēmisomnus	half-asleep
10	semper	always
11	senātor: senātōrem	senator
5	senex: senem	old man
	senior	older, elder
	sēnsim	slowly, gradually
	sententia	opinion
12	sēnsit	felt
	serpēns: serpentem	snake
10	servat: servāvit	saves, looks after, preserves
1	servus	slave
	sibi	to himself
4	signum	sign, seal, signal

8	silva	woods, forest
	sine	without
11	sollicitus	worried, anxious
10	sōlus	alone, lonely
	sonuit	sounded
	sonus	sound, noise
	sordidus	dirty
	soror: sorōrem	sister
8	spectāculum	show, spectacle
5	spectat: spectāvit	looks at, watches
	spectātor: spectātōrem	spectator
	spīna	thorn
	spīrat	breathes
	splendidus	splendid
5	stat	stands
8	statim	at once
	statua	statue
	stēlla	star
	stertit	snores
	stilus	pen, stick
	stola	(long) dress
11	stultus	stupid
	stultior	more stupid
	stultissimus	very stupid
	suāviter	sweetly
6	subitō	suddenly
	sum	I am
	sumus	we are
	sunt	they are
6	superat: superāvit	overcomes, overpowers
	superfuit	survived
3	surgit: surrēxit	gets up, rises
	suscipit	undertakes, takes on
	susurrāvit	whispered, muttered
10	suus	his, her, their
	Syrius	Syrian

t

3	taberna	store, shop, inn
	tablīnum	study
10	tacet: tacuit	is silent, is quiet
7	tacitē	quietly, silently
7	tamen	however

12	tandem	*at last*	
	tantum	*only*	
	tē	*you* (singular)	
	tēcum	*with you* (singular)	
12	templum	*temple*	
	tenet	*holds*	
12	terra	*ground, land*	
7	terret: terruit	*frightens*	
	tertius	*third*	
	testis: testem	*witness*	
	tetigit	*touched*	
	theātrum	*theater*	
	thermae	*baths*	
	tibi	*to you* (singular)	
12	timet: timuit	*is afraid, fears*	
	timidē	*nervously*	
	titulus	*notice, slogan*	
	toga	*toga*	
	tondet	*shaves, trims*	
	tōnsor: tōnsōrem	*barber*	
8	tōtus	*whole*	
9	trādit: trādidit	*hands over*	
	trahit: trāxit	*drags*	
	tremor: tremōrem	*trembling, tremor*	
	tremuit	*trembled, shook*	
12	trēs	*three*	
	triclīnium	*dining room*	
	trīgintā	*thirty*	
	trīste	*sadly*	
	trīstis	*sad*	
4	tū	*you* (singular)	
	tuba	*trumpet*	
6	tum	*then*	
	tunica	*tunic*	
5	turba	*crowd*	
	turbulentus	*rowdy, disorderly*	
	tūtus	*safe*	
6	tuus	*your, yours*	

u

5	ubi	*where*	
	ubīque	*everywhere*	
	ululat: ululāvit	*howls*	

	umbra	*ghost, shadow*	
12	ūnus	*one*	
5	urbs: urbem	*city*	
	ūtilis	*useful*	
	ūtilissimus	*very useful*	
10	uxor: uxōrem	*wife*	

v

	vāgīvit	*cried, wailed*	
7	valdē	*very much, very*	
11	valē	*good-bye*	
10	vehementer	*violently, loudly*	
	vēnābulum	*hunting spear*	
	vēnālīcius	*slave dealer*	
	vēnātiō: vēnātiōnem	*hunt*	
	vēnātor: vēnātōrem	*hunter*	
6	vēndit	*sells*	
5	venit: vēnit	*comes*	
11	verberat: verberāvit	*strikes, beats*	
	versipellis: versipellem	*werewolf*	
	versus	*verse, line of poetry*	
	vertit	*turned*	
	vexat	*annoys*	
1	via	*street*	
	vibrat	*waves, brandishes*	
	victor: victōrem	*victor, winner*	
3	videt: vīdit	*sees*	
	vīgintī	*twenty*	
	vīlicus	*farm manager*	
	vīlla	*villa, house*	
3	vīnum	*wine*	
11	vir: virum	*man*	
	vīsitat	*visits*	
	vīta	*life*	
6	vituperat: vituperāvit	*tells off, curses*	
	vīvit	*is alive*	
	vōbīs	*to you* (plural)	
4	vocat: vocāvit	*calls*	
10	vōs	*you* (plural)	
	vulnerāvit	*wounded, injured*	

Index of cultural topics

actors 58, 60, 64–66, 79, 160
aediles 49, 153, 159–162
amphitheater 24, 34–36, 79, 102, 109, 159–160
Anaximander 137
animal hunts 36, 112
apodyterium 124–129
aqueduct 35
archaeology 8, 175–177
architects 81, 175
arena 109, 112, 160
armor 110–111
atrium 11–13, 23–24
Augustus 78
awning 65, 109

basilica 34, 46, 50–51
baths 13, 23–24, 34–35, 115, 119, 124–130, 159
Bay of Naples 8, 174
bestiarii 112
business 8–9, 13, 23, 35–36, 38, 48, 50, 78, 81, 107, 144–145, 160–161

caldarium 125–127, 129
Campania 8, 33, 113, 174
candidatus 35, 81, 154–155, 159–161
cena 21, 24–25, 80, 87
clan 9–10
clientes 23, 81, 159–160
compluvium 11
cooking 24–26, 48, 79, 145
cubiculum 11–12, 15
culina 11, 13, 26

drama 64–67
duoviri 159

education 24, 143–145
elections 9, 35, 37, 49–50, 64, 81, 145, 154–155, 159–162
emperors 34, 48, 50–51, 78, 113, 159–160
Epicurus 97
Eumachia 34, 48, 50–51
Euripides 137

family 9–13, 24, 48, 50, 66, 95–97, 144, 159, 161, 177
fauces 11
Flacci 159
forum 23, 34–35, 39, 43, 46, 48–51, 64, 125–129, 144, 155, 159-160
freedmen and freedwomen 23, 65, 78, 80–82
frigidarium 127–129

gladiators 36, 79, 99, 103, 107, 109–111, 113–114, 160–161
gods 11–13, 38, 50, 68, 141, 167, 169
government 35–36, 50, 159–160
graffiti 37, 49, 65, 160–162
grammaticus 144
Greeks 36, 65, 96–97, 129, 137, 143–145

Herculaneum 8, 34, 49, 75, 95–97, 115, 124, 127, 130, 174–177
Holconii 147, 159–160
Homer 144
Horace 144
hortus 10–11, 13, 24, 32, 58, 79, 81, 97, 177
household 2, 10–11, 23, 32, 50, 80, 145, 167
houses 8–13, 34–35, 37, 78–81, 95, 97, 126, 129, 175, 177
hypocaust 129

ianua 11–12
impluvium 11–12
Isis 50, 169, 175
Ixion 98

jewelry 14, 23, 44, 96, 141, 169, 175–177
Juvenal 66

lararium 11–12, 50, 167
Lares 34, 50–51, 167
latrina 11, 13, 34

law 9–10, 46-47, 49–50, 78, 80, 137, 143, 145, 159–160
life after death 95–98
Lucian 96
ludi magister 143, 145

makeup 23, 177
manumission 69, 80
marriage 10, 66, 78, 81, 145
masks 53, 58, 60, 65–67
meals 23–25, 177
mosaics 6, 12, 65, 67, 79, 83, 87, 89–90, 106–107, 114, 124, 130, 137, 145, 179
municipal offices 50–51
murmillones 110–111
music 50, 65, 67, 79, 107, 109, 145

names 9–10, 34, 78, 81
Nero (emperor) 113, 160
Nola 8, 34
Nuceria 8, 34, 95, 113, 160

paedagogus 143
painting 12–13, 21, 25, 27, 29, 32–33, 35–38, 47–49, 53, 60, 66, 68, 76, 82, 86, 107, 109, 113, 143–144, 146, 159, 161, 163, 173, 175, 177
palaestra 34, 36, 119, 126, 128–129
pantomime 65
papyrus 143–144, 146
patronus 23
peristylium 11–13, 81, 126
Plautus 66–67
Pompeii 8, 10-13, 33–38, 48–52, 64–65, 113, 124–127, 156–160, 174–178 and *passim*

Regulus 113, 160
retiarii 103, 110–111, 114
rhetor 131, 145
riot at Pompeii 113
rooms (names of) 11–13

schools 143–145
Seneca 128
shops 8, 11, 13, 24, 34–35, 37–38, 43, 49–50, 64, 75, 79, 81, 122, 129
Sisyphus 98
slaves 8–10, 13, 23–24, 31, 35, 64–67, 69, 78–81, 110, 126, 143, 145, 176
Sorex 64–65
Stabiae 8, 34, 36, 174
stilus 143, 146
stola 23
streets 11, 33–38, 49, 79, 159, 161
strigil 126

tablinum 11–13, 177
tabulae 9, 47, 143–144, 146, 177
Tacitus 113
Tantalus 98
temples 24, 34, 50–52, 79, 81, 154, 160, 169, 175
tepidarium 126–127, 129
Terence 66
theaters 24, 36, 64–67, 79, 81, 159–160, 174
toga 23, 159
tombs 95–97
town council 50, 64, 79, 81, 159–160
triclinium 11–13, 24, 82, 90, 97
tunic 23

Vesuvius 8, 24, 33–34, 109, 163, 173–174
Vettii 81–82
Virgil 144–145

water supply 35, 159
wine 24, 37, 68, 96
women 10, 14, 24, 48, 64–67, 81, 96, 109–110, 125, 128–130, 145, 161, 176
writing 9, 143–146

Index of grammatical topics

accusative case 21, 32, 104, 120–121, 182–183, 191
adjectives 191
    see also   comparative
             superlative

cases
    see   accusative case
          dative case
          nominative case
comparative 140
conjugations 185, 187
conjunctions 190

dative case 120–121, 152, 182–183, 189
declensions 32, 62, 121, 182, 191

imperfect tense 74–75, 172–173, 184–186

main clauses 190

nominative case 21, 32, 62, 104, 120–121, 182–183, 191
nouns 21, 32, 62, 182–183, 191
number
    see   plural
          singular

perfect tense 74–75, 90, 172–173, 184–185, 187–188, 191–192
person 59–60, 87, 138, 184, 191
plural 59–60, 62, 74–75, 90, 104, 121, 138, 172, 182–184, 186
present tense 7, 74–75, 90, 138, 184–188, 191–192
pronouns 45, 121, 138, 152, 172

questions 156

singular 45, 59–60, 62, 74–75, 90, 104, 121, 172, 182–184, 186, 191
subject omitted from sentences 87, 189
subordinate clauses 190
superlative 107

tenses
    see   imperfect tense
          perfect tense
          present tense

verbs
          irregular 7, 45, 60, 75, 138, 172, 186
          regular 7, 45, 59, 74–75, 138, 172, 184–188, 191–192

word order 7, 21, 189

Time chart

Date	Pompeii	Rome and Italy
BC *c.* 3000		
c. 3000–332		
c. 2100		
c. 1750		
c. 1500		
c. 1250		
c. 922		
753		Rome founded (traditional date)
c. 700–600	Greek merchants settle	
c. 530	Etruscans control Pompeii	
509		Kings expelled/Roman Republic begins
c. 525–400		
474	Samnites capture Pompeii	*Duodecim Tabulae*, 450
390		Gauls capture Rome
300–200	Romans defeat Samnites	Rome controls Italy/Wars with Carthage
218		Hannibal crosses the Alps
200–100	Temple of Isis built	Rome expands outside Italy
133–123		Gracchi and agrarian reforms
90–80	Pompeii becomes a Roman colony	Cicero, Roman orator (106–43)
58–49		
44		Julius Caesar assassinated
27		Augustus becomes emperor
70–19		Virgil, author of the *Aeneid*
15	Major public works program	
AD 14		Tiberius becomes emperor
41		Claudius becomes emperor
43		
59	Pompeians and Nucerians riot	Nero emperor (54–68)
62–63	Earthquake damages Pompeii	Great Fire at Rome/Christians persecuted
69–79	Amphitheater restored	Vespasian emperor
c. 72		Colosseum begun
79	Last elections, March	Titus becomes emperor
79	Vesuvius erupts, late summer or fall	Tacitus, historian (*c.* 56–117)
81		Domitian becomes emperor
98–117		Trajan emperor
117		Hadrian becomes emperor
313		Constantine supports toleration of Christianity
330		
c. 385		Bible translated into Latin

World history	World culture	Date
Babylonian/Sumerian civilizations		BC *c.* 3000
Pharaohs in Egypt		*c.* 3000–332
Indo-European migrations	Maize cultivation, American SW	*c.* 2000
Hammurabi's Legal Code	Epic of Gilgamesh	post 2000
Minoan civilization at its height	Rig-Veda verses (Hinduism) collected	*c.* 1500
Israelite exodus from Egypt	Development of Hinduism	*c.* 1450
Israel and Judah split	Phoenician alphabet adapted by Greeks	*c.* 1000–800
Kush/Meroe kingdom expands	*Iliad* and *Odyssey*	*c.* 800
	First Olympic Games	776
Solon, Athenian lawgiver, 594	Buddha	*c.* 563–483
	Confucius	551–479
	Golden Age of Greece	500–400
Persia invades Egypt and Greece	Death of Socrates	399
Conquests of Alexander the Great		335–323
	Museum founded in Alexandria	290
Great Wall of China built		*c.* 221
Judas Maccabaeus regains Jerusalem	Feast of Hanukkah inaugurated	165
	Adena Serpent Mound, Ohio	2nd C
		106–43
Julius Caesar in Gaul	Canal locks exist in China	50
	Glassblowing begins in Sidon	post 50
Cleopatra commits suicide		30
Herod rebuilds the Temple, Jerusalem		*c.* 20
Roman boundary at Danube	Birth of Jesus	*c.* 4
	Crucifixion of Jesus	AD *c.* 29
	St Peter in Rome	42–67
Britain becomes a Roman province	St Paul's missionary journeys	45–67
	Camel introduced into the Sahara	1st C
		64
Sack of Jerusalem and the Temple		70
Roman control extends to Scotland		77–85
	Paper invented in China	*c.* 100
		79
	Construction at Teotihuacán begins	*c.* 100
Roman empire at its greatest extent		98–117
Hadrian's Wall in Britain		122–127
"High Kings" of Ireland		*c.* 200–1022
Byzantium renamed Constantinople	Golden Age of Guptan civilization, India	*c.* 320–540
	Last ancient Olympic Games	393

Date	Pompeii	Rome and Italy
410		Alaric the Goth sacks Rome
476		Last Roman emperor deposed
590–604		Gregory the Great, pope
800–1100		Period of turmoil in Italy
850		Republic of St Mark, Venice
1066		
1096		
1143–1455		Independent government in Rome
1271–1295		Marco Polo travels to the East
1265–1321		Dante, author of *La Divina Commedia*
c. 1400		Renaissance begins in Italy
1445–1510		Botticelli, painter
1453		
1492		Titian, painter (1489–1576)
1506		Rebuilding of St Peter's begins
1508		Michelangelo starts Sistine Chapel ceiling
1527		Rome sacked by German and Spanish troops
1530–1796		Spain controls much of Italy
1534		
1594	Fontana rediscovers Pompeii	
1610		Galileo invents the telescope
1620		Bernini, architect and sculptor (1598–1680)
1644–1912		
1682–1725		
1748	Excavations for treasure	
c. 1760		
1776		
1796		Napoleon enters Italy
1813–1901		Verdi, composer
1824		
1848–1861		Mazzini, Garibaldi, Cavour, Italian patriots
1860	Fiorelli excavates systematically	
1861		Victor Emmanuel II, king of a united Italy
1861		
1872		
1896		Marconi invents wireless telegraphy
1914–1918		
1918		
1922–1945		Mussolini controls Italy
1944	Vesuvius erupts again	
1946		Italy a republic

World history	World culture	Date
Mayan civilization		*c.* 300–1200
Byzantine empire expands		518
	Birth of Muhammad	570
Charlemagne crowned, 800	Arabs adopt Indian numerals	*c.* 771
Vikings reach America, *c.* 1000	*1001 Nights* collected in Iraq	ante 942
Norman invasion of England	*Tale of Genji*, Japan	1010
First Crusade	Ife-Benin art, Nigeria	1100–1600
Magna Carta, 1215	Classic Pueblo Cliff dwellings	1050–1300
Genghis Khan (1162–1227)	Al-Idrisi, Arab geographer	1100–1166
Mali empire expands, 1235	Arabs use black (gun) powder in a gun	1304
Joan of Arc dies, 1431	Chaucer's *Canterbury Tales*	ante 1400
Inca empire expands, 1438	Gutenberg Bible printed	1456
Turks capture Constantinople	Building at Zimbabwe	*c.* 15th C–*c.* 1750
Columbus arrives in America, 1492	Vasco da Gama sails to India	1497–1498
	Martin Luther writes *95 Theses*	1517
		1519–1522
Cortez conquers Mexico		
Mogul dynasty established	Magellan names Pacific Ocean	1520
	Copernicus publishes heliocentric theory	1543
French settlements in Canada	Shakespeare	1564–1616
Burmese empire at a peak	Muskets first used in Japan	*c.* 1580
Continuing Dutch activity in the East	Cervantes publishes *Don Quixote*	1605
Pilgrims land at Plymouth Rock, 1620	Taj Mahal begun	1632
Manchu dynasty, China	Palace of Versailles begun	1661
Peter the Great rules Russia	Newton discovers the Law of Gravity	1682
	J. S. Bach, composer	1685–1750
Industrial Revolution begins, *c.* 1760	Mozart, composer (1756–1791)	*c.* 1760
American Declaration of Independence	Quakers refuse to own slaves	1776
French Revolution begins	Washington, US President	1789
Napoleon defeated at Waterloo	Bolivar continues struggle, S. America	1815
Mexico becomes a republic	S. B. Anthony, women's rights advocate	1820–1906
American Civil War, 1861–1865	Communist manifesto	1848
Lincoln emancipates American slaves		1863
Canada becomes a Dominion	French Impressionism begins	1867
Serfdom abolished in Russia	Mahatma Gandhi	1869–1948
Cetewayo becomes king of the Zulus	Edison invents phonograph	1877
	First modern Olympic Games	1896
First World War, 1914–1918	Model T Ford constructed	1909
Bolshevik Revolution in Russia	Bohr theory of the atom	1913
	US Constitution gives women the vote	1920
Second World War		1939–1945
United Nations Charter		1945